© Kristin Dean and Emma Mathlin, 2025

The moral rights of the author have been asserted.

All rights reserved. Except as permitted under the Australian Copyright Act 1968 (for example, a fair dealing for the purposes of study, research, criticism or review), no part of this book may be reproduced, stored in a retrieval system, communicated or transmitted in any form or by any means without prior written permission.

All inquiries should be made to the author.

Disclaimer
The material in this publication is of the nature of general comment only and does not represent professional advice. It is not intended to provide specific guidance for particular circumstances and it should not be relied on as the basis for any decision to take action or not take action on any matter which it covers. Readers should obtain professional advice where appropriate, before making any such decision. To the maximum extent permitted by law, the author and publisher disclaim all responsibility and liability to any person, arising directly or indirectly from any person taking or not taking action based on the information in this publication.

ABOUT US

Emma & Kristin

Founded by Kristin Dean (human/equine physiotherapist) and Emma Mathlin (human/equine physiotherapist and sports scientist), Equimotion is an Australian company providing physiotherapy, rehabilitation and biomechanics for horse and rider.

Equimotion is driven by a commitment to advancing the well-being of horses, with a strong clinical focus on education and exercise prescription. We work with owners at the grassroots level, all the way up to elite athletes, in the pleasure, performance, racing and breeding fields.

We believe in working with riders and owners to develop management plans together – taking into account their goals, expectations and abilities. Our goal is to give owners the knowledge and tools to take an active role in their horse's ongoing care. It's often the consistency and effort from the owner that has the greatest impact on injury prevention and long-term soundness.

Emma and Kristin are both riders, giving them a comprehensive understanding of horse and rider biomechanics and training. Emma grew up competing in eventing and now enjoys working with her Irish sport horse Jack, as well as retraining OTTBs. In years past, Kristin trained and competed in dressage. She now enjoys riding mainly for pleasure when she can fit it in between work and ferrying her kids around to sport and other activities!

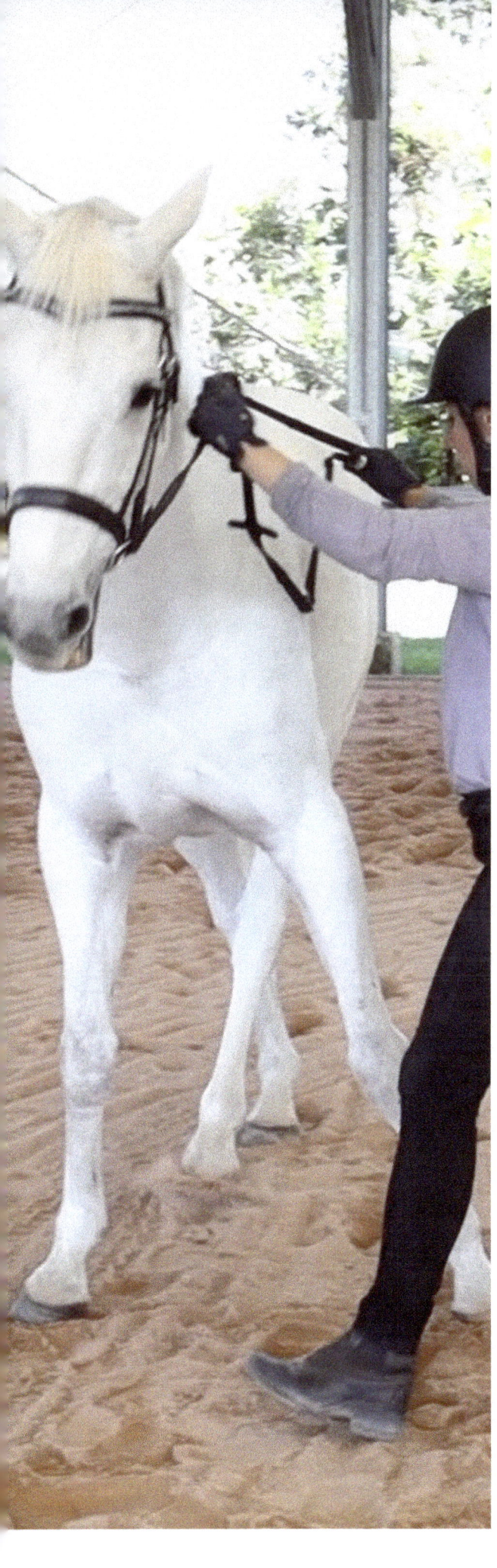

CONTENTS

04
Who Is This Book For?

05
How To Use This Book

06
Getting To Know Your Horse

15
Chapter 1: Understanding Your Horse's Training Needs

25
Chapter 2: Exercise Prescription Principles

53
Chapter 3: Load Management

82
Chapter 4: Monitoring For Early Signs of Injury

91
Chapter 5: Understanding The Effects of Exercise and Training Practices

122
Chapter 6: Back and Neck Care

147
Chapter 7: The Horse-Rider Relationship

153
References

161
Index

WHO IS THIS BOOK FOR?

As physiotherapists, we encounter a lot of horses experiencing pain and injury. In many cases, these issues could have been prevented. The owners of these horses aren't neglectful or uncaring, on the contrary most are deeply committed to their horses' well-being. More often than not, they simply lacked the knowledge necessary to recognise the subtle signs that something was wrong.

Historically, the horse industry has faced gaps in education on key topics such as managing training loads, understanding the effects of different exercises, speed and surfaces, recognising signs of subtle pain, promoting recovery, and appreciating the influence of the rider on the horse. Thankfully, these areas are gaining increased attention, with many people now acknowledging that understanding these principles is crucial to manage a sound and healthy horse.

As awareness grows, the volume of information available can be overwhelming, and it's not always clear where to turn for trustworthy advice. Outdated perspectives still persist, with dismissive phrases such as "she's just being a chestnut mare" or "work him through it" commonplace. If your instincts tell you otherwise, and you're eager to learn more to help your horse stay sound and injury-free, this book is for you.

With many years of combined experience in equine and human physiotherapy, we've refined our knowledge and skills to address these challenges.

This book is written to guide you in structuring training and exercise programs that reduce your horse's risk of injury. It will help you develop training skills that enhance strength, posture, and movement patterns so you can support your horse's health and performance.

HOW TO USE THIS BOOK

While it might be tempting to prescribe a one-size-fits-all approach to exercise and training, such as "do these exercises, this many times, for every horse", the reality is far more nuanced. Every horse is, and needs to be treated as, an individual. Equally, as an owner or rider, your goals, capabilities and available resources also need to be considered. What we offer in this book is a clear understanding of the principles of exercise prescription and training. Our aim is to equip you with the knowledge to design tailored training programs that can help minimise the risk of injury and optimise your horse's performance.

In physiotherapy, we use a process called clinical reasoning to guide our treatment plans. Clinical reasoning involves gathering information from the patient (or the owner, in the case of animals), processing this information to understand the underlying problem, planning and implementing interventions, evaluating outcomes, and reflecting on the entire process to inform future decisions. This is similar to the process we all engage in regularly during our daily lives when solving problems or completing tasks. As riders, adopting this can be invaluable in planning and structuring an effective training regime for your horse.

The focus of this book is to provide you with a framework of reasoning skills to guide you through the creation of a training program tailored to your horse's unique needs. This framework covers key areas such as:
- understanding why overuse injuries occur
- understanding foundational exercise and training principles
- learning how to manage training loads to avoid injury
- assessing and monitoring your horse
- incorporating rest and recovery periods
- tools and techniques to measure performance
- understanding the impact of different exercises and the rider's influence on the horse

We have also included several case studies to illustrate these concepts in practice. It's important to emphasise that the training programs we present in these examples are not meant to be universally applied. Instead, they serve to demonstrate our reasoning process by explaining the choices made, why they were made, and how the specific needs of both horse and rider were factored into the overall plan.

We base our advice on the most up-to-date research and as such we have referenced numerous studies in this book. Rather than provide all the references in the text (and make the book feel like a stuffy textbook!), we have instead provided a list of the papers we mention at the end of the book for your reference. You will also find QR codes throughout the book that will link to videos of many of the exercises. These are on our exercise prescription software, EQ Active, which is a tool for equine practitioners to prescribe exercise programs to their clients.

GETTING TO KNOW YOUR HORSE

In this book we talk a lot about the different parts of your horse. We describe the anatomy of the lower limb, neck and back and their relevance to training your horse in more detail later in the book. Some of the other common terms and areas of the body that we will refer to and are important to understand in relation to training your horse are detailed below.

The thoracic sling

Unlike a human, the horse doesn't have a collarbone. This means that there is no bony attachment of the forelimb to the rest of the skeleton. The horse instead has the thoracic sling, a group of muscles which provide the sole connection between the forelimb and the trunk. As such, they play a crucial role in the horse's balance and movement. The muscles that make up the thoracic sling are trapezius, serratus ventralis, subclavius and pectorals.

When the forelimbs are on the ground, contraction of both sides of the thoracic sling muscles together lift the sternum and withers, helping to shift the horse's weight back onto the hindquarters. Contraction of the muscles on just one side of the body influence straightness and position of the shoulders. We will discuss straightness in more detail in Chapters 1 and 2.

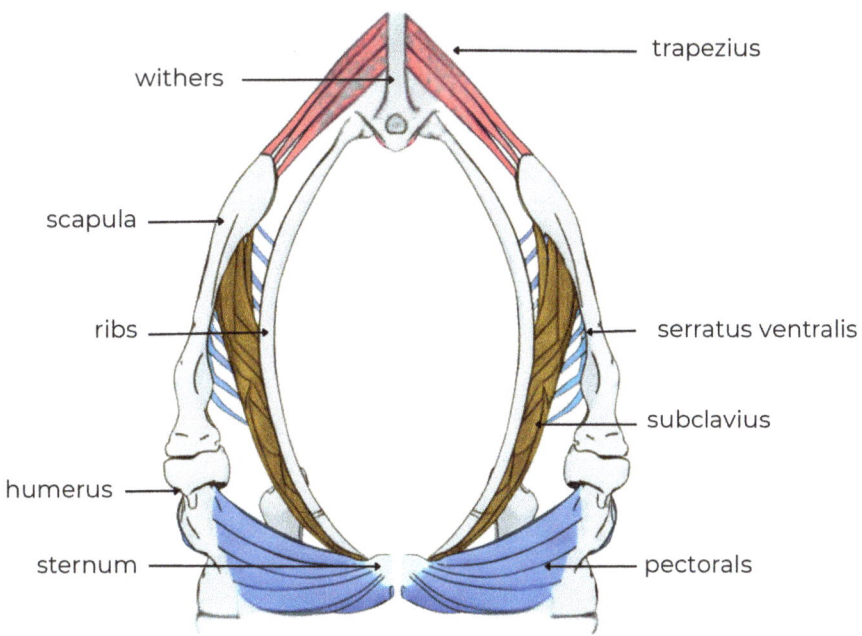

GETTING TO KNOW YOUR HORSE

The pelvis

The pelvis is made up of three bones that are fused together – the ilium, ischium and pubis. It connects the spine to the hindlimbs and is essential for providing stability, serving as a major attachment point for the hindquarter muscles. What is often referred to as the point of the hip is actually part of the pelvis called the tuber coxae. The hip joint sits lower and deeper, attaching the thigh bone to the lower part of the pelvis.

The sacroiliac joint (SIJ) is the connection point between the pelvis (ilium) and the spine (sacrum). It is through this joint that forces from the hindlimbs are transmitted to the spine, transferring high loads through it at speed. A common misconception about this region is that a horse's pelvis or hip can "go out" of alignment. This is simply not true. Both the SIJ and hip joints are very stable joints, supported by a large number of ligaments and covered by exceptionally large and strong muscles. Neither joint can simply slip out of position. If this were to occur, it would be a veterinary emergency and your horse would not be able to walk!

There is actually very little movement at the SIJ, with research showing there is only 1-3 degrees of movement. The joint's main role is to provide stability, not mobility. In some horses you may notice an asymmetry of the pelvic bones. This doesn't mean that the pelvis is out of alignment. Asymmetry can occur if the horse has suffered a bony injury in the past, such as a pelvic fracture, which can lead to a structural change in bone shape. Tears to the ligaments supporting the SIJ can also lead to bony asymmetry of the tuber sacrale, which are the top points of the pelvis. Asymmetry can also simply be due to a structural difference in the size and shape of the bones between left and right that the horse is born with. It is, of course, important to monitor any asymmetry in your horse, and speak to your vet if you have any concerns or notice a change in function.

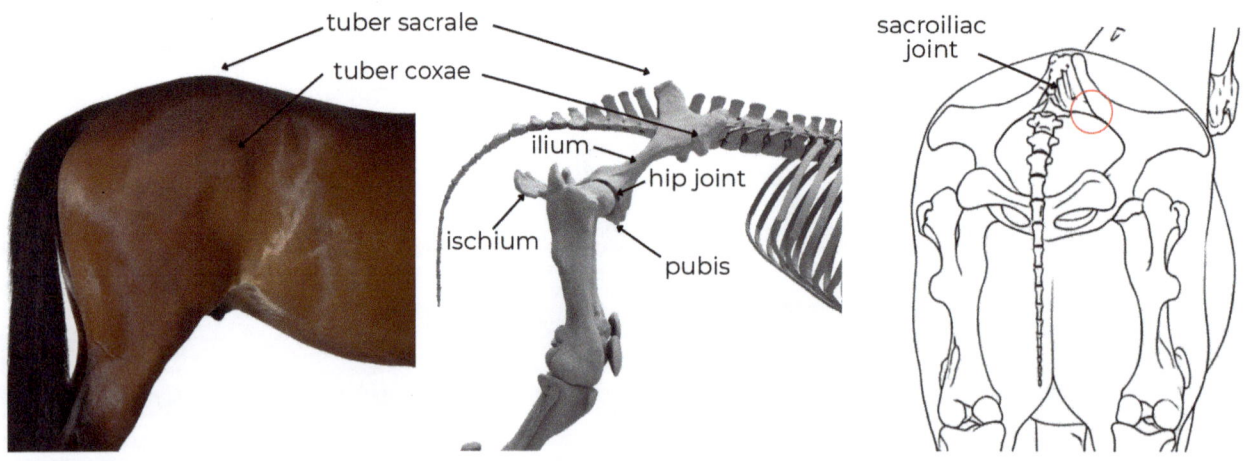

You will note in the image above how deep the sacroiliac joints are. These joints are covered in large amounts of muscle.

GETTING TO KNOW YOUR HORSE

The hock

The hock is made up of 6 different bones and is equivalent to the ankle joint in a human. It consists of 4 joints: the tibiotarsal joint, the proximal intertarsal joint, the distal intertarsal joint, and the tarsometatarsal joint. It is found in the hindlimbs only.

The hock is designed to absorb shock, and to flex (bend) and extend (straighten). Flexion allows the horse to bring their hindlimbs up and forward underneath the body, and extension helps with hindlimb propulsion or push off. Most of the flexion and extension takes place in the upper part of the hock, which is the tibiotarsal joint. Behind the talus, a bone called the calcaneus sits to form the point of the hock. This acts like a brace to prevent the hock from hyperextension.

In the lower part of the hock sit the four tarsal bones, forming the proximal intertarsal joint, the distal intertarsal joint, and the tarsometatarsal joint. The joints in this section of the hock have limited range of motion, with their main function being shock absorption.

We share a case study about a horse with pain in both their hock and sacroiliac joints in Chapter 4.

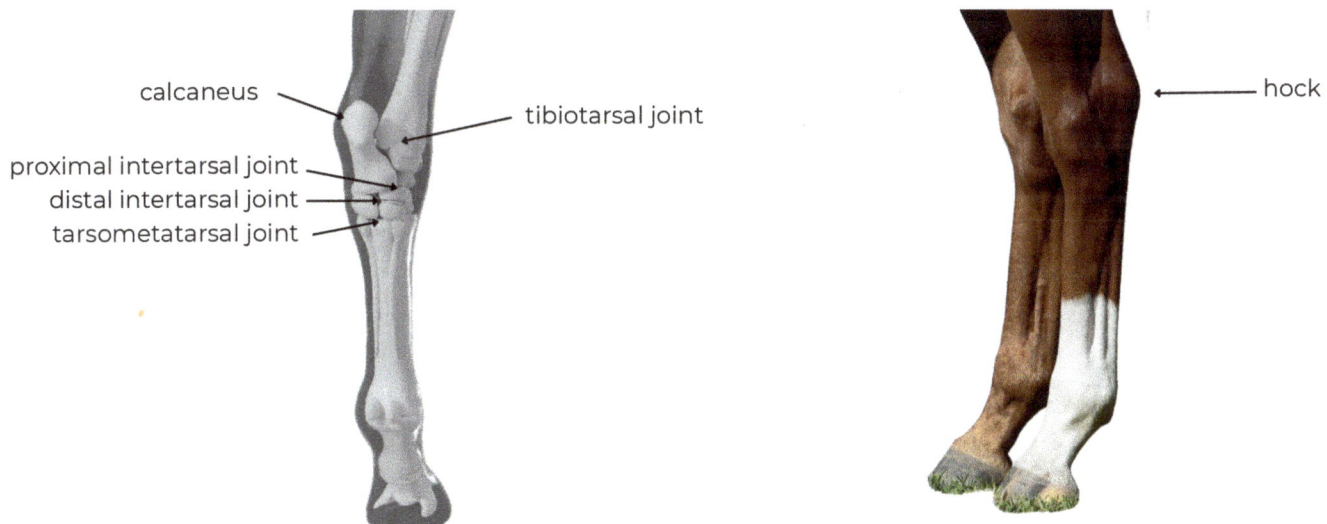

GETTING TO KNOW YOUR HORSE

The fetlock

The fetlock is a joint in the lower limb of each leg, sitting between the canon bone, the proximal sesamoid bones and the long pastern bone. It has the greatest amount of movement of any joint in the horse's body, moving in a flexion and extension direction (opening and closing the angle the angle between the cannon bone and the pastern) and plays a pivotal role in locomotion. It absorbs a huge amount of force when the horse's limb is in contact with the ground, particularly at high speeds and on landing from a jump. The soft tissues around the joint are stretched during this contact phase, absorbing and storing energy. This energy is released during during propulsion, aiding efficient movement. As such, the joint and surrounding soft tissues are highly susceptible to injury. We will detail these soft tissues and their role in supporting the fetlock joint further in Chapter 2.

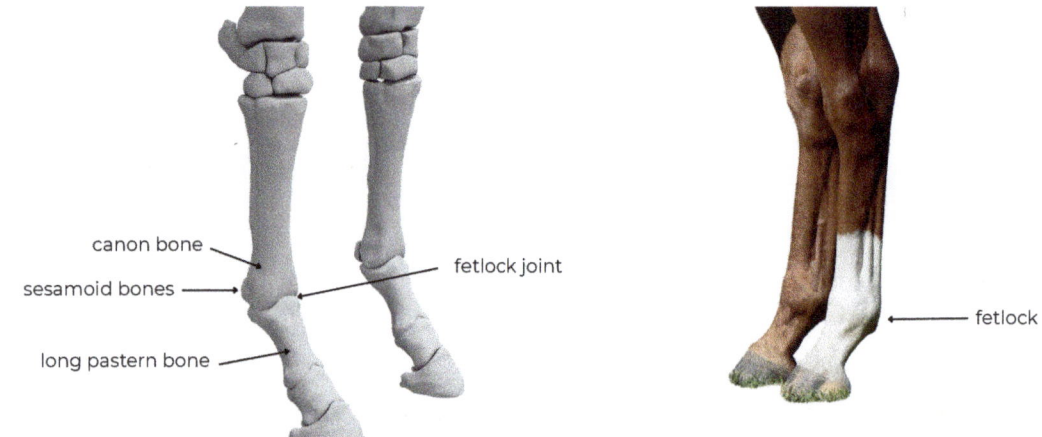

Muscles

We will reference a number of different muscles throughout the book. Here is a simple reference guide to highlight where they are located on the horse. We detail the anatomy of the lower limb in Chapter 3 and the back and neck in Chapter 5.

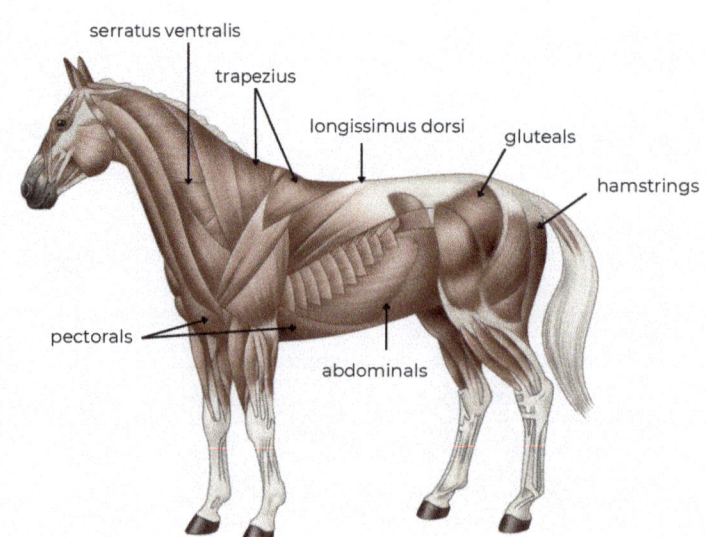

GETTING TO KNOW YOUR HORSE

The hoof

No hoof, no horse. We've all heard this saying, and it's definitely true. Whilst it is beyond the scope of this book to cover the hoof in detail, it's important to understand how it can have a significant impact on the rest of the horse's body, in particular joints and soft tissues. It is essential to consider your horse's hooves when it comes to training and injury management practices.

The hoof is much more than the external hoof wall, sole and frog that we can see. Internally, there is a complex arrangement of bones, joints, tendons and ligaments. The main bone inside the hoof wall is the distal phalanx, or the coffin bone. The shape of this bone mirrors the hoof wall. Directly above the distal phalanx is the middle phalanx (short pastern) and the proximal phalanx (long pastern) bones. These three bones form the coffin and pastern joints, which are essential for mobility, locomotion and shock absorption. There is an additional small bone at the back of the foot called the navicular. The function of the navicular bone is to serve as a surface for the deep digital flexor tendon to slide over.

Supporting the bones and joints are a number of tendons and ligaments. We discuss the digital flexor tendons and suspensory ligament in more detail in Chapter 3. The deep digital flexor tendon (DDFT) runs over the top of the navicular bone and inserts into the underside of the coffin bone. Injuries to this tendon are common and can be career limiting (or even ending in some cases). The ligaments that surround the coffin and pastern joints are called the collateral ligaments. Injury can occur to these ligaments when the hoof is placed under high loads from twisting (such as when circling or on a soft surface) or when the horse slips or slides (such as can occur in a paddock injury). The distal sesamoidean impar ligament (often called the impar ligament) connects the navicular bone to the coffin bone and helps provide stability to the navicular bone, limiting excessive movement. It plays a key role in distributing forces during weight-bearing and breakover. Injuries to this ligament are often associated with navicular related lameness.

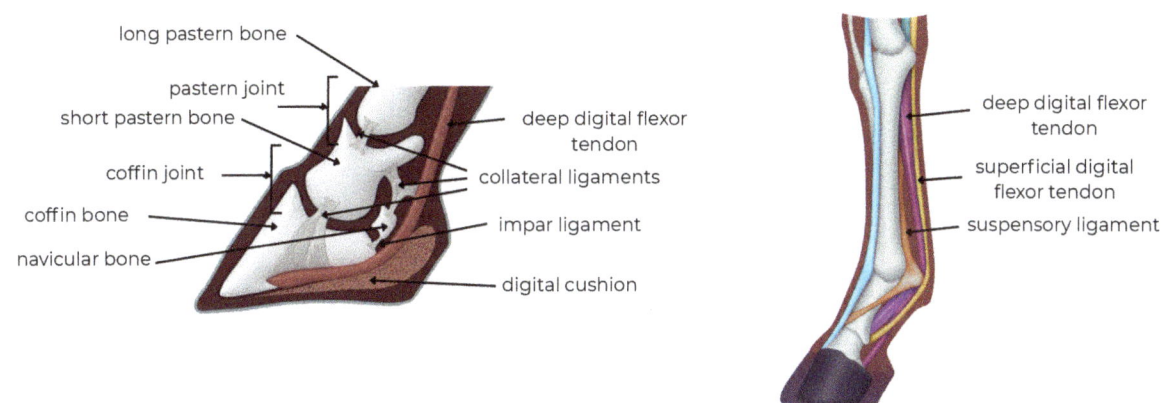

GETTING TO KNOW YOUR HORSE

The hoof is a neurosensory organ, full of nerves that provide sensory and proprioceptive feedback to the brain. This allows the horse to perceive changes in terrain and surface and adjust posture and movement accordingly.

Hoof balance

Hoof balance refers not only to the shape and alignment of the hoof, but how the hoof lands and supports the horse's weight during movement. Getting this right helps to ensure that the impact forces generated when the hoof hits the ground are centred and evenly distributed. This is vital, as uneven loading has been shown to have direct links to increased risk of lameness and injury.

Palmar/plantar angles (PA)

The palmar angle (front feet) and plantar angles (hind feet) refer to the angle of the coffin bone relative to the ground. Ideally, this angle should be slightly positive (typically between 2-10°). It's suggested that a positive palmar or plantar angle ensures that forces through the hoof are directed and distributed evenly. A negative palmar or plantar angle (NPA) is however, a common finding, particularly in the hind feet. This means that back of the coffin bone sits lower than the front, a position often linked to long toe-low heel foot conformation. Research has found that a NPA places excessive stress on the deep digital flexor tendon, the navicular bone and associated soft tissues, increasing the risk of injury to these structures.

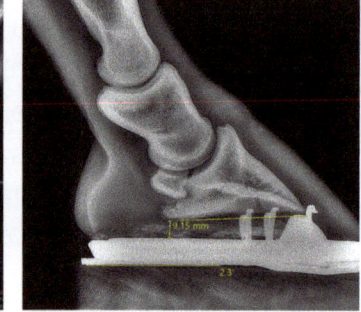

An example of a positive palmar angle (left) and negative palmar angle (right).

Research has also found that improving a NPA in the hindfeet can also change a horse's posture. A canted-in posture refers to a stance in which the horse's hindlimbs are brought further forward underneath their trunk, creating a non-vertical alignment of the limb. This posture was found to be improved with farriery intervention improving plantar angles.

Heel to toe ratio

The heel to toe ratio refers to toe length and heel height. This ratio determines the horse's breakover, which is the point in the stride where the heel lifts and the toe pivots off the ground. An ideal breakover allows for optimal movement, allowing the hoof to pivot quickly and efficiently over the toe, minimising the time the limb is subjected to high forces. A long toe and low heel conformation significantly increases the lever arm on the foot. This prolongs the breakover, as the hoof has to rotate over a greater distance, causing the foot to stay in contact with the ground for longer and increasing the force around the coffin joint. This translates to increased strain on the tendons, especially the DDFT.

Pastern-hoof alignment

This refers to the alignment of the hoof wall to the pastern bones. It is easy to observe as a visual line when you look at your horse's limb from the side. A perfectly straight or aligned angle is the goal, however a common finding is the "broken-back" angle, where the hoof angle is too shallow compared to the pastern. This angle is closely related to the heel to toe ratio, with a broken-back alignment commonly resulting from a long toe and low heel conformation. Correct and regular trimming (with therapeutic farriery intervention in some cases) is essential to restore and maintain ideal ratios and alignment.

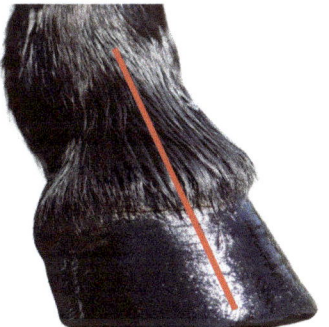 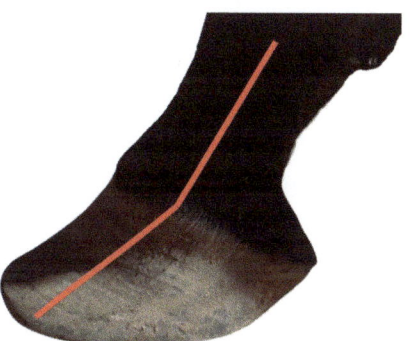

A straight pastern-hoof alignment (left) and an example of a broken back alignment, with a long toe and low heel (right).

Effect of poor hoof balance on the body

Poor hoof balance can have widespread effects on the horse's body, and it needs to be closely monitored and maintained to help minimise the risk of injury. As mentioned previously, a negative plantar angle can change the way the horse stands, which can result in compensatory postural changes in the neck and back. Altered limb loading is another consequence of poor hoof balance. If forces are distributed unevenly during stance and gait, it can overload different structures. Medial-lateral (or side-to-side) imbalances can place extra stress on the collateral ligaments and may increase concussion forces. Inflammation in the coffin joint bursa, asymmetry during swing or stance of a limb, mechanical laminitis, and hoof capsule deformation are all potential outcomes, often causing compensatory adjustments elsewhere in the body.

GETTING TO KNOW YOUR HORSE

The way a horse lands also affects tissue and joint health. Landing toe-first can create shear forces in the soft tissues of the feet, and uneven landing creates further stresses up the limb, impacting the coffin, pastern, and fetlock joints. Over time, these forces can contribute to chronic musculoskeletal issues.

Hoof Imbalance	Biomechanical Effect	Injury Risk
Long toe/low heel	Delayed breakover, DDFT tension	Navicular syndrome, DDFT strain/injury
Medial-lateral imbalance	Uneven load, altered centre of rotation	Joint asymmetry, collateral ligament strain
Collapsed heels	Poor shock absorption	Digital cushion degeneration, laminitis
Negative Plantar Angles (hind)	Tucked-under posture, back tension	SIJ pain, back strain, hock/stifle pain/injury
Toe-first landing	Altered shock absorption	Suspensory ligament & flexor tendon injuries

Owner management

It's important to note that every horse is different and, like people, no two horses will have exactly the same feet. Hoof balance is also dynamic and changeable – environment, conformation, work/training, feeding and housing all have an effect. You will find that your horses hooves may change many times over their lifetime. It's important to remember:

- Corrections can take time and require incremental change. Trying to make drastic changes to your horse's feet in one trimming cycle can cause more issues than it helps.
- Teamwork is essential – ensure your vet, farrier, physio and any other veterinary professionals helping your horse all work together.
- Regular farrier consultations are essential, and should occur every 4-6 weeks.
- Take regular photos of your horse's feet on flat even ground (from the side and in front) to monitor any changes. This can be really helpful for your vet and farrier.
- Train on a variety of good quality surfaces to help improve proprioceptive input.

An excellent resource is Hoof Care with the Equine Documentalist by Yogi Sharp, available on the Ridely app.
https://app.ridely.com/en/training-programs/hoof-care-with-the-equine-documentalist

GETTING TO KNOW YOUR HORSE

Hoof balance checklist

Please seek advice from your vet and farrier if any of the following apply to your horse.

1. Visual Hoof Inspection (Standing on Flat Ground)

Check	What's Healthy	Warning Sign
Toe length	Short, proportionate toe	Long toe ('ski slope' look)
Heel height	Upright, solid, not crushed	Low, under-run, collapsed heel
Hoof symmetry (front view)	Both sides of hoof look equal	One side steeper/flatter (sheared heels)
Frog contact	Frog contacts ground slightly (barefoot)	Frog recessed or atrophied
Hoof-pastern axis	Straight line from pastern into hoof	Broken-back (dropped toe), broken-forward (clubby)
Shoe placement (if shod)	Shoe ends just behind heel bulbs	Shoe too far forward or pinched under heel

2. Movement & Gait

Check	What's Normal	Warning Sign
Landing	Flat or slightly heel-first	Toe-first landing, stabbing stride
Stride length	Even, fluid	Short-strided, especially in hind limbs
Turning	Willing, balanced turns	Resists turning, especially on hard ground
Tracking up	Hind hoof steps into/over front track	Hind hoof steps short

3. Postural Red Flags (When Standing)

Check	What's Normal	Warning Sign
Hind limb alignment (side view)	Cannon bones vertical or near-vertical	Hind legs 'canted-in' (tucked under)
Front limb posture	Even weight distribution	Standing with one foot consistently forward/back
Topline appearance	Relaxed, level back	Hollow back, lack of/uneven muscle development

4. Handling the Hoof

Check	What's Normal	Warning Sign
Heel bulbs	Firm, even	Contracted, narrow, sensitive
Digital pulse	Soft or hard to find	Strong/bounding pulse = inflammation
Sole wear pattern	Even on both sides	Uneven wear, excessive toe wear, flares
Frog & sole condition	Dry, rubbery, clean	Black thrush, overly soft, crumbly or recessed frog

Chapter 1

UNDERSTANDING YOUR HORSE'S TRAINING NEEDS

Aligning training with discipline to reduce injury risk

TRAINING NEEDS

How discipline-focused training supports your horse's wellbeing

Every discipline places unique demands on the horse's body. From the endurance required of an eventer, the explosive power of a showjumper and the strength displayed by a dressage horse, training must reflect these specific demands to keep the horse sound and performing well. If your training isn't aligned with the individual needs of your horse, they may be underprepared for the stress placed on their body, leading to poor performance and increased risk of injury. Understanding and implementing discipline-specific training needs ensures horses are well-prepared for their work.

The main physical components to be trained are as follows. Most horses will require a number of these to be considered in their training programs.

- **Aerobic fitness**: Improving cardiovascular stamina for sustained effort over time.
- **Endurance:** Increasing the horse's capacity to perform for long periods without fatigue. This is important for long rides or events spanning multiple rounds, hours or days.
- **Strength**: Improving the horse's ability to generate force, as needed with high level collected movements or tackling steep terrain.
- **Power:** Enhancing muscular force production, for example clearing a large jump or quick bursts of speed.
- **Mobility or suppleness:** Improving flexibility and range of motion.
- **Straightness / symmetry:** Encouraging the horse to use both sides of the body equally, minimising uneven loads that can lead to injury.
- **Proprioception**: Improving body awareness and the horse's ability to adjust to footing, terrain, or balance challenges.
- **Motor control / skill development:** Refining coordination and precision of movement, essential for executing complex tasks like high-level dressage movements or navigating technical jump courses.

TRAINING NEEDS

Aerobic/cardiovascular training

Aerobic fitness refers to how well the heart, lungs and circulatory system can take in and utilise oxygen to perform exercise. A horse with good aerobic fitness is able to perform exercise for longer and at a higher intensity than a horse with poor fitness, who might huff and puff excessively with low level activity. It is required for any discipline that involves sustained effort, especially where horses need to perform for longer than a few minutes at a time.

Key examples include:
- Endurance – relies heavily on aerobic capacity to cover long distances in trot and canter.
- Eventing (cross-country phase) – requires high, sustained energy output over several minutes at speed.
- Showjumping (long courses or multiple rounds) – aerobic fitness is needed to ensure that the horse recovers well between rounds and avoids fatigue, which is crucial to maintain form over fences.
- Dressage – though not a high-intensity discipline when compared to others, aerobic fitness is required to perform a full test accurately and without fatigue.
- Trail riding – relies on aerobic fitness to sustain effort over long periods, often across varied terrain.
- Racing (especially longer-distance races) – sprint races place higher demands on anaerobic systems, longer races (such as steeplechase or those over 2-3km) require a high level of aerobic fitness.

While aerobic fitness is essential for the disciplines mentioned above, all horses benefit from training it. Good aerobic fitness helps minimise fatigue, enhances recovery between training sessions, and supports overall wellbeing. These are essential elements to minimise the risk of injury and keep your horse performing well.

Anaerobic fitness refers to the body's ability to perform short, high-intensity activities (for example sprinting). The energy systems used do not require oxygen. Fatigue occurs quickly and activity can only be maintained for short periods of time (less than 2 minutes).

TRAINING NEEDS

Endurance

Endurance is the ability of the body (both musculoskeletal and cardiovascular systems) to work over time without excessive fatigue. Training for endurance leads to physiological adaptations that enhances efficiency of the body, allowing the horse to perform the same workload at a lower relative intensity.

Endurance is a combination of aerobic fitness and muscular endurance. A horse with good muscular endurance is one that is strong enough to sustain activity, and maintain form and posture for long periods. Fatigue leads to poor biomechanics (such as toe dragging and tripping), which can increase the risk of injury.

Key examples include:
- Endurance – the most extreme example, where horses may cover up to 160 km in a single day.
- Racing – long-distance races, such as the Melbourne Cup (in which horses travel 3.2 km in about 3 minutes), require both aerobic capacity and muscular endurance. Fatigue in such a race can be catastrophic.
- Trail Riding / Hacking – endurance is needed to undertake extended periods of walking, trotting and cantering over varied terrain.
- Eventing – sustained cantering/galloping (combined with jumping) demands both aerobic fitness and muscular endurance to complete the course safely and within time limits. A high level of endurance also helps the horse recover well between phases, and perform three different disciplines back to back (dressage, cross-country and showjumping) in either one or consecutive days.

TRAINING NEEDS

Strength

Strength is the ability to withstand or exert force. Strength training helps the horse's muscles, tendons, ligaments, and bones adapt so they can cope with the demands of work. It also improves the ability of the muscles to generate enough force to perform the movements or tasks required of the discipline.

Key examples include:
- Dressage – considerable strength is required to perform collected and high-level movements, such as piaffe, passage, pirouettes, and flying changes.
- Jumping / Eventing – strength, particularly of the trunk and hindquarters, is necessary to generate the force required to clear fences safely and efficiently.
- Driving / Draft Work – a prime example of strength requirement in the horse. Driving horses need the ability to produce and maintain muscular strength to pull heavy loads.
- Endurance / Trail Riding – strength is necessary to maintain balance whilst navigating uneven terrain and inclines, along with the ability to maintain a steady gait over prolonged periods.

Power

Power is the ability to produce force quickly. Training for power focuses on explosive movements where a large amount of force is generated in short bursts.

Power training helps horses develop the ability to accelerate, change pace, or produce sudden, high-intensity efforts. It is especially important in disciplines that require quick bursts of speed or dynamic changes in movement.

Key examples include:
- Showjumping / Eventing – requires the ability to generate power during jump take-off.
- Racing – both jumping out of the barriers and accelerating down the track relies heavily on power.
- Dressage – transitions from collected to extended paces demand short bursts of power.
- Western Disciplines (Barrel Racing, Reining, Cutting) – quick accelerations, sliding stops, and rapid directional changes require powerful muscular engagement.

TRAINING NEEDS

Flexibility

Flexibility refers to how a horse's muscles and joints move through their full range of motion. The degree of flexibility varies between horses, but all require a baseline level to maintain joint health and whole-body movement. Factors such as genetics, age, activity level and past injuries can all influence range of motion.

Many people assume poor flexibility comes from "tight muscles". In reality, it is more commonly linked to restricted joint range of motion (such is as commonly seen in arthritic joints), and reduced muscular strength. When it comes to training flexibility, it is therefore necessary that mobility and strength training go hand in hand.

At the other end of the spectrum, some horses can display hypermobility, which is when joints display an unusually large range of motion. While this is often seen as desirable, particularly in horses with expressive and large moving paces, it can cause issues. While research in horses is limited, human studies have shown that hypermobility can increase injury risk. Too much mobility, particularly in horses that may lack strength and control, places extra stress on the soft tissues, making them more susceptible to injury.

Key examples include:
- Dressage – often the main discipline considered when it comes to mobility, horses require good flexibility to perform lateral movements equally on both reins.
- Jumping – good flexibility in the spine and limbs allows the horse to clear fences safely, along with absorbing the high forces of landing.
- Western – a high degree of flexibility is required for sliding stops, spins and tight turns.
- Racing – good mobility of limbs, back and neck is crucial for stride length and efficiency.

TRAINING NEEDS

Proprioception

Proprioception is the horse's awareness of where its body and limbs are in space. A horse with good proprioception will place its feet accurately, adjust well to changes in surface and terrain and maintain their balance during movement.

The aim of training proprioception is to improve how well the horse's nervous and musculoskeletal systems work together to coordinate movement. It is something that is often considered in rehabilitation, but it should be developed in all training programs, for all horses. It helps improve coordination and agility, reducing the risk of trips, falls and soft tissue strain.

Key examples include:
- Eventing / Endurance / Trial Riding – any discipline that involves travelling over varied and uneven ground requires good proprioception.
- Jumping – limb placement and balance during all phases of the jump (approach, take-off, flight and landing) rely on strong proprioceptive ability.
- Western – with slides, spins and turns performed at high speed, having a horse who is aware of where its limbs are is crucial for safety and performance.
- Racing – when travelling at high speeds in a tight group, lacking proprioception can lead to serious injury, for the horse themselves, their jockey and the horses / jockeys they are racing against.
- Polo – proprioception is vital for quick direction changes and maintaining balance as the rider shifts their position in the saddle.

TRAINING NEEDS

Symmetry and Straightness

Straightness

According to the FEI training scale, straightness is defined as:
"When the horse's forehand is in line with its hindquarters, that is, when its longitudinal axis is in line with the straight or curved track it is following."

In practice, straightness refers to the horse's ability to move in a balanced, rhythmical manner with the hindfeet tracking directly in line with the forefeet, and the ability to bend and flex equally on both reins. Achieving true straightness requires correct training that develops strength, suppleness, and the equal use of both sides of the body.

Straightness is crucial for both performance and physical health:
- In competition: Dressage scores are awarded for equal performance on both reins; jumping horses must be able to take off, land, and turn in both directions.
- For physical health: A straight horse distributes its weight evenly across both sides of the body, pushes off equally from both hind limbs, and absorbs ground reaction forces evenly through all four limbs.

Symmetry

Symmetry, on the other hand, refers to a physical state. In both humans and animals, bilateral symmetry is the concept that the body's two halves are mirror images when divided down the centre. While perfect symmetry is rare, striving for near-symmetry can help ensure even force distribution across the body, potentially reducing wear and tear, and lowering injury risk.

Asymmetry is any difference between the left and right sides of the body. It can be structural, such as a difference in the size, shape or position of a bone from side to side, a difference in size or shape of the hooves, or pelvic asymmetries due to previous injury. These cannot be altered. There may also be differences in symmetry due to functional factors, such as strength, mobility or proprioception. Functional factors arise from how the horse uses its body, such as favouring one lead, pushing off more strongly with one hindlimb or having a preferred direction of bend. Unlike structural asymmetries, functional factors can be addressed and symmetry improved with targeted training. Asymmetry can arise from various sources, such as:
- congenital (present at birth)
- trauma or injury
- uneven conditioning or training
- handling habits (e.g., always saddling and mounting from the same side)

TRAINING NEEDS

When does asymmetry become lameness?

A sound horse moves with symmetrical limb loading and movement patterns. Horses can have minor gait asymmetries or slight differences in left to right sided movement patterns that are not clinically relevant or cause an issue to the horse.

Lameness is a clinical sign of pain, mechanical restriction or altered neuromuscular function causing an altered stance or gait. Asymmetric limb loading and movement patterns are seen in lameness that are associated with pathological processes. The lame horse is unwilling or unable to stand or move normally and there can be many different causes. Lameness is only able to be diagnosed by the treating veterinarian, and its presence always warrants assessment. See Chapter 4 for more information on detecting asymmetrical gaits.

Human athletic symmetry and injury risk

Although it is a complex relationship, some asymmetries in human athletes have been linked to a greater risk of injuries such as ACL tears, hamstring strains and ankle sprains. It is thought that differences in strength, mobility or balance can lead to injuries due to uneven workloads or excessive stress on one limb. We should note that not all asymmetries in human athletes are detrimental, especially in sports with one dominant limb such as tennis or kicking sports.

When training horses, it is reasonable to aim for improvement of significant asymmetries in functional factors such as strength, mobility, coordination and movement biomechanics to lower the risk of injury due to uneven loads.

Body balance

It's also important to evaluate the balance of the body, not just from left to right, but also front to back. This includes comparing the neck, shoulders, and forelimbs to the hindquarters and hindlimbs. Some horses have overdeveloped neck and shoulder areas compared to their hindquarters and tend to pull themselves along rather than pushing from behind, potentially overloading the tissues of the forelimbs. We can also examine the muscle balance between the topline and the underside of the body. An example is a horse with overdevelopment of the under neck muscles who may travel with their head up in the air and an extended back posture, potentially resulting in the development of back pain.

TRAINING NEEDS

Motor control/skill development

Motor control is the horse's ability to coordinate its body to produce even and balanced movement. A horse requires good motor control before they can refine the specific movement patterns and skills needed for their discipline. Consistency and correct training practices are key in developing motor control and skill.

Training motor control helps improve balance, coordination and proprioception. A horse with good motor control is less likely to trip or move unevenly, minimising the risk of injury. While some disciplines require greater control than others, motor control underpins all safe movement, especially in tasks such as stepping over poles, carrying a rider and negotiating uneven ground.

Having a good understanding of the skills required for your horse's discipline is essential. It is necessary to break down the components of a skill in order for the horse to not only learn it, but also develop the fitness, strength, power, endurance and/or proprioception it needs. We will cover this in more detail in Chapter 2.

Key examples include:
- Dressage – finely tuned motor control is required for transitions, lateral work and collected movements. A high degree of skill needs to be developed as the horse progresses through the levels. In the next chapter, we will demonstrate how to break down a complex skill, such as a pirouette, to train it more effectively.
- Jumping – clearing the fence is only one small component of the skill. The horse needs to have the ability to gauge distances, adjust their stride length and coordinate their body during take-off and landing.
- Western – across a number of western disciplines, the horse needs the control and skill to be able to perform precise movements such as sliding stops, spins and quick directional changes. Such movements require refined control and timing.

Chapter 2
EXERCISE PRESCRIPTION PRINCIPLES

Planning your training to minimise the risk of injury

EXERCISE PRESCRIPTION PRINCIPLES

Designing an effective training program goes far beyond choosing the right exercises. It is similar to cooking, it relies on understanding the elements and steps needed to achieve the desired result. When you cook, you don't throw random ingredients and measurements together and hope for the best! Putting together a training program is exactly the same, you need to determine what to do, how to do it and when to do it. In training, this is called the FITTP principle:

FREQUENCY, INTENSITY, TIME, TYPE, PROGRESSION

Frequency

Frequency refers to how often the exercise/s are completed. This may be how many times per day or per week.

An integral part of any training program is ensuring that, in addition to scheduling exercise days, you also include recovery/rest days. This allows the tissues to adapt to the stress of exercise.

Intensity

Intensity refers to how hard the session is. An example of a low-intensity session may be a walk hack out or a short lunging session that includes only a few minutes of trot. A high-intensity session could involve time spent at high speeds, incorporating discipline specific training such as jumping, learning a new skill in dressage or generally stepping up training to a new height or level.

Intensity can be measured using a heart rate monitor or GPS to determine speed and time spent in each gait. Examples of apps and products that allow you to do this include:
- KER Clock It
- Equilab
- Equisense

It can also be measured using a RPE scale (rating of perceived exertion). The rider applies a number along a scale of how hard they determine the horse found the session. This has been found to correlate strongly with measured heart rate in humans. We will explain this in detail in Chapter 3.

Time

Time refers to the duration of the exercise or session.

There is an inverse relationship with duration and intensity of the session. Higher intensity sessions require a shorter time duration, whereas lower intensity sessions can be longer.

EXERCISE PRESCRIPTION PRINCIPLES

Type

Type refers to the specific exercise/s you perform.

Examples of this may be strength, mobility/stretching, endurance, power, balance or proprioception.

Progression

Progression refers to how you move to the next stage of the training program. In order to make continual improvements, progression is required. This may involve:

- Moving from simple to more complex movements, e.g., simple leg yield to shoulder-in and travers.
- Increasing resistance or load, e.g., moving from long lining/lunging to adding a rider.
- Increasing the intensity, e.g., increasing speed, adding in a slope or changing surface.
- Increasing the duration or frequency.

Most of these factors will have a direct relationship with the others and it's important to increase only one variable at a time. For example, if you increase your intensity, your frequency of performing that exercise should initially decrease, along with the duration of the exercise.

Once you understand the FITTP principles, how do you know how to apply them in practice? *The first thing you need to do is to determine the aim of the exercise* – whether it's to build aerobic capacity, endurance, strength, power, flexibility, straightness, proprioception, motor control, or a combination of these.

We can think about prescribing exercise like medicines with a 'dosage'. Dosage refers to the total amount of exercise and is made up of the FITTP principles described above. For example, when you take paracetamol for a headache, half a tablet is unlikely to have an effect, whereas 20 tablets will result in overdose. The optimal dose for most people is likely to be 1-2 tablets.

We need to take the same approach when designing training programs, ensuring each exercise is prescribed at the right type, intensity, and duration to achieve its specific aim. Too little exercise will be unlikely to achieve improvements, while too much can potentially lead to injury. Like medicine, people (and horses) may respond to exercise dosage slightly differently, so it is important to prescribe an exercise dosage to each horse and monitor their individual responses to ensure optimal training load.

EXERCISE PRESCRIPTION PRINCIPLES

Aerobic prescription

Aerobic exercise dosage is determined by intensity, frequency, and duration. These should be gradually increased, with only one variable changed at a time. All horses beginning or returning to training after spell should have initial phases incorporating longer durations of slow speed work early in their preparation, while the later phases of training can include durations of higher-intensity work.

Measuring heart rate combined with speed is the most simple and reliable way to measure and monitor aerobic fitness. A mature horse's resting heart rate can sit between 25-40 beats per minute (bpm), reaching up to a maximum of 220-240 bpm with high-intensity exercise. Each horse has their own individual maximum heart rate that reduces slightly as they age. It can be used as a guide to gauge fitness and exertion, as a horse that is able to sustain higher speeds at the same maximum heart rate is considered to be fitter. A heart rate range of 140-170 bpm during exercise is a good indicator of a horse working aerobically (with oxygen); a zone where improvements in aerobic fitness can be gained. When heart rates reach higher than around 170bpm, a horse will start to work anaerobically (without oxygen). Work cannot be sustained for long periods of time above these heart rates, so shorter bursts of higher intensity activity need to be interspersed with lower intensity recovery periods. The higher the intensity of activity, the shorter the duration of training is completed.

Heart rate training zones

Zone	% or Heart Rate Max	Goal of training
Very Light	30-60% of HR max (up to 140bpm)	Warm-up, active recovery, rehabilitation
Light	60-70% (up to 160bpm)	Basic training, basic aerobic endurance
Moderate	70-80% (up to 180bpm)	Moderate aerobic training
Hard	80-90% (180-200bpm)	Strenuous training, high speed endurance, anaerobic power
Maximum	90-100% (200-240bpm)	Sprint training, anaerobic capacity

Data referenced from Polar White Paper 2013

EXERCISE PRESCRIPTION PRINCIPLES

A lower heart rate measured at the same speed over subsequent training sessions typically shows that the horse is improving its aerobic fitness. For example, an eventing horse completes two fitness training sessions per week. In the first week of fitness training, the horse canters at a speed of 450 metres/second for six minutes with a heart rate of 200bpm. During the third week of training, the horse completes the same canter speed with a heart rate of 185bpm, showing an improved physical tolerance of the training load. It's important to measure this consistently and regularly though, as a horse's heart rate can fluctuate if something in their environment causes them stress or excitement.

Note that aerobic fitness gains can be made in 8-12 weeks of training, whereas musculoskeletal strengthening, especially tendons and ligaments, takes much longer to achieve.

If you'd like to learn more about structuring training sessions for aerobic conditioning, we suggest the following resources:

- Conditioning Sport Horses by Hilary Clayton
- The Athletic Horse: Principles and Practice of Equine Sports Medicine by David Hodgson and Reuben Rose
- Ask your vet – many are trained to carry out or interpret these tests and can help apply them to your horse.
- Look for online webinars or courses on equine fitness – several vet and physio or exercise physiologist-led programs offer owner-friendly explanations and examples. Dr David Marlin is a great online resource.

Heart rate recovery is an important measure of how well a horse is coping with exercise demands. The horse's heart rate should start to lower when exercise stops. Fit horses ridden to their level of ability/fitness level should show a recovery of less than 50% of their peak heart rate during that exercise session within 15 minutes. Peak heart rate is the highest heart rate the horse reached during that ride, not their absolute maximum (which is usually around 220 bpm for most horses). So, if your horse hit 180 bpm during the session, you'd want to see it drop to 90 bpm or less within 15 minutes.

Equine heart rate monitors are readily available and are quite easy to use on your horse during training sessions. They can be an effective tool to measure and monitor how your horse is responding to your training sessions, and can alert you to times when you may need to seek veterinary advice or make adjustments to your training program.

EXERCISE PRESCRIPTION PRINCIPLES

Why you should measure aerobic fitness and when to seek help

Regular monitoring of your horse's heart rate can help you detect signs of fatigue and ensure optimal performance. If the heart rate reaches abnormally high levels or if it fails to return to normal levels fairly soon after exercise, it can indicate an issue with your training and/or highlight a problem that requires veterinary attention.

Significant and out of the ordinary variations in the horse's heart rate may be signs of a cardiac or respiratory issue, or another underlying health problem. Research (and the reported clinical experience of many vets) shows that heart rate can increase in cases where a horse is lame or experiencing an episode of laminitis. Vets will often advise that they observe changes in heart rate before the issue is obvious on clinical examination.

Heart rate variations during exercise and recovery can also reveal whether your training load is appropriate for your horse and your training / competition goals. A consistently elevated heart rate and long recovery times may suggest overtraining, increasing the risk of injury. Equally, a lack of aerobic challenge, as seen with consistently low heart rates during training, could leave your horse underprepared for competition or a sudden increase in training demands.

Some of the products on the market at time of publication (and that have been validated in research studies) include Polar Equine Heart Rate Monitors and Equimetre by Arioneo. We recommend you speak to your vet or other equine professional for assistance in selecting, setting up and using a heart rate monitor in your training.

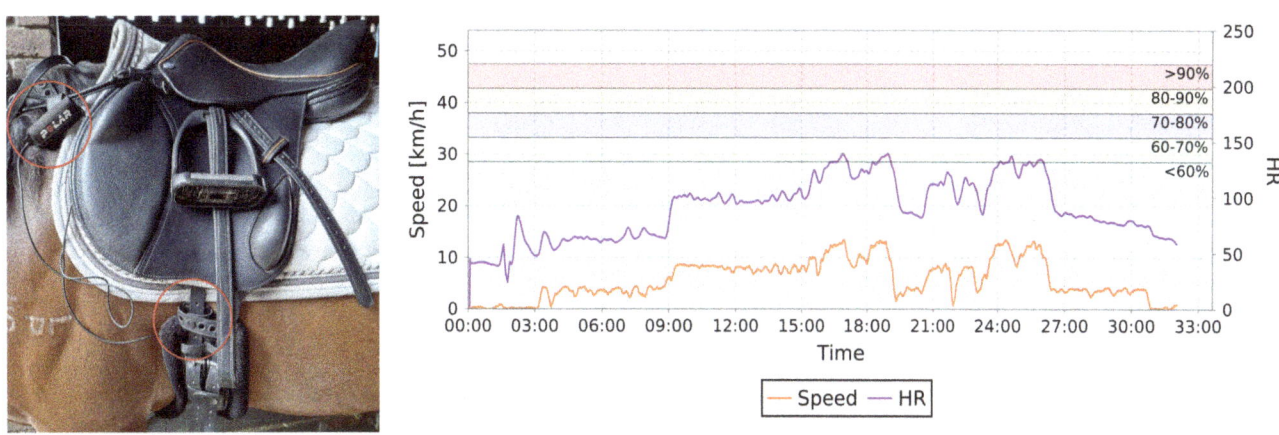

The Polar equine heart rate monitor attached to the saddle (left). The Bluetooth receiver (top circle) allows you to follow the horse's heart rate or record data to analyse later with any Bluetooth-compatible Polar sports watch or on your phone (via the Polar Equine App or KER Clockit Sport). The heart rate sensor sits on left side of girth. HR tracking graph (right). This was collected during a ridden conditioning session (flatwork on sand arena). The horse spent the majority of the session below 50%, 6 minutes between 50-60% and 2 minutes at 60-70% (this was during canter). Overall this was a low-intensity aerobic session.

EXERCISE PRESCRIPTION PRINCIPLES

Sample Training Session – Aerobic Focus

Goal: Elementary level dressage horse has had sporadic work over the last few months and now needs to increase her aerobic fitness base to improve her general conditioning for a competition in 8 weeks time. She is slightly overweight and puffs quite a lot with canter work. The rider is increasing the number of training sessions per week to 4, and is including a general aerobic session aimed to increase her ability to cope with her work without fatiguing. The following session was conducted with a heart rate monitor. The horse was found to be working in the 50-60% HR maximum zone for the trot work and 60-70% zone for canter.

- Warm-up (15 mins)
    - Active walk with shoulder-in, leg-yield, and transitions
    - Stretching trot with frequent changes of rein

- Main Set – Continuous work
    - Trot 10 mins (forward, working trot)
    - Walk 3 mins (active)
    - Canter 6 mins (3 min each lead)
    - Walk 3 mins (active)
    - Trot 10 mins (forward, working trot)

- Cool-down (10 mins)
    - Loose rein free walk

EXERCISE PRESCRIPTION PRINCIPLES

Interval training

Another method of training fitness is to perform sport-specific movements in an interval training format. Interval training involves alternating short, high-intensity bursts of moderate-high intensity exercise with lower intensity recovery phases throughout a single training session. This type of training may help to improve both muscular strength and power, along with aerobic fitness and muscular endurance.

High-intensity interval training (HIIT) involves short bursts of hard exercise, at about 80% or more of maximum effort, followed by rest periods. Typically, the rest period is the same duration as the exercise (e.g., perform canter for one minute, then walk for one minute, repeated 4-6 times). Sprint interval training (SIT) is even more intense. It uses very short, all-out efforts that go beyond what the body can maintain for long, followed by longer rest periods (e.g., 15–20 second gallop at maximum effort, followed by a 4–5 minute walk or slow trot for full recovery, repeated 4 to 6 times).

It's been found that both high-intensity interval training (HIIT) and sprint interval training (SIT) in Thoroughbreds led to greater improvements in strength and fitness compared to moderate-intensity continuous training (MICT), even when exercise volumes were the same. MICT means performing the exercise continuously at a moderate intensity level (e.g trotting for 15 minutes without stopping). Researchers found that HIIT and SIT induce more intense physiological responses and trigger greater adaptations in skeletal muscle, leading to enhanced endurance, muscle strength, and overall fitness levels.

It's important to note that horses trained with HIIT and SIT require an excellent aerobic and musculoskeletal conditioning first, gained with lower intensity continuous training, in order to cope with the higher intensity and forces involved in high intensity interval training.

EXERCISE PRESCRIPTION PRINCIPLES

Sample Training Session – Interval Training Showjumper

Goal: Within 10 weeks, improve the amateur showjumping horse's ability to complete multiple competition rounds with a speed jump-off, reducing rails knocked down by 50% and consistently meeting time limits.

- Warm-Up (20 mins)
    - 10 mins active walk: shoulder-in, leg-yield, walk–halt–walk transitions
    - 5–7 mins rising trot: large circles, serpentines
    - 3 mins canter (each lead)

- Main Set – Interval blocks
    - Set 1: Flat-based intervals (repeat 3-4 rounds):
        - 3 min working trot around arena
        - 3 min working canter around arena
        - 2 min collected canter short sides → lengthened canter down long sides
        - 1 min walk
    - Purpose: Build postural endurance and heart rate conditioning with tempo variation.

    - Set 2: Jump-integrated intervals (repeat 2–3 rounds)
        - Canter small course of 4–6 fences
        - Walk 3–4 min to full recovery
        - Optional: Include trot pole grid before re-jumping to test focus under fatigue
    - Purpose: Simulates short-course jumping effort followed by recovery demand.

- Cool-Down (10-15 mins):
    - Walk on long rein

EXERCISE PRESCRIPTION PRINCIPLES

Endurance prescription

Endurance is improved by training with higher volumes of exercise at lighter loads or lower intensities. Greater than 15 reps or a longer time duration is usually appropriate. A shorter duration rest period between sets of exercises is required as the intensity of the exercise is lower and recovery faster. Exercise examples include hydrotherapy (such as swimming or walking through water), mid-long duration trot or canter sessions, or long-distance trails.

It is important to consider the job that is required of the horse and the fitness parameters required for that job. This will inform you of how to best prescribe reps/sets/duration that will be targeting the correct fitness parameter.

> **Sample Training Session – Endurance Focus**
>
> **Goal:** Improve an endurance horse's ability to maintain a steady trot at 13 km/h for at least 20 km without signs of fatigue, within 6 weeks.
>
> - Warm-up (10 mins)
>   - Active walk
>
> - Main Set – Sustained Effort (e.g. field or XC-type track)
>   - Trot: 20 mins on varying terrain (steady, ground-covering)
>   - Canter: 8 mins (forward seat)
>   - Walk: 5 mins (active recovery)
>   - Repeat trot/canter set x 2
>   - Option: include technical terrain (e.g. small banks, footing changes)
>
> - Cool-down (10 mins)
>   - Active walk

EXERCISE PRESCRIPTION PRINCIPLES

Sample Training Session – Return to Work / Low Level Trail Riding Focus

Goal: 20 year old ex-eventer coming out of retirement needs to improve general cardiovascular fitness and muscular endurance in order to complete 2 x 45 minute trail rides per week

- **Warm-up (10 mins)**
    - 5 min loose rein walk, encouraging relaxation and stretching
    - 5 min walk / halt / walk / trot transitions

- **Main set (25-30 mins)**
    - Trot: 8 mins on easy terrain (steady rhythm, relaxed frame, ridden in a light seat)
    - Active Walk: 5 min recovery
    - Trot: 8 mins on slightly varied footing and inclines (e.g., grass, dirt – surface will be regularly working on)
    - Active Walk: 5 min recovery
    - *Note: no canter yet – building foundational fitness first*

- **Cool-down (10 mins)**
    - Loose rein walk, encourage lowering of head and neck

EXERCISE PRESCRIPTION PRINCIPLES

Strength prescription

For effective improvements in strength to occur, strength training is typically performed three days per week, allowing for rest/recovery days between sessions. Research in humans shows that untrained people may gain strength benefits with one session per week, whilst trained individuals may require three or more training sessions weekly to continually gain increases in strength.

When planning how to structure an exercise session, we often talk about reps, sets, and duration:
- Reps (short for repetitions) = how many times your horse does the movement in a row (e.g., stepping over a pole 10 times = 10 reps).
- Sets = how many times you repeat that group of reps, with a short rest in between. For example, 10 reps × 3 sets means your horse does the movement 10 times, rests, and repeats that group of 10 movements twice more.
- Duration = how long the movement is done for, if it's held or continuous (e.g., walking up a hill for 20 seconds, or holding a posture, such as a long and low frame, for one minute).

In order to follow strength prescription principles, perform fewer than 8 reps or a short duration (10–20 seconds) when the load or intensity is high. Perform 8–15 reps or a slightly longer duration (20–30 seconds) for moderate load or intensity. Complete 3–5 sets, with a rest period of 1-3 minutes between sets to allow for recovery.

EXERCISE PRESCRIPTION PRINCIPLES

Sample Training Session – Strength Focus

Goal: 8 year old horse competing well at novice level would like to step up to compete in an elementary test in 8 weeks time. The horse needs to improve their ability to perform more collected paces in trot and canter.

- Warm-up (15 mins)
    - Walk lateral work in a slightly stretched frame
    - Walk/trot transitions, serpentines and figure-8s

- Main Set
    - Hill reps (slow tempo, encourage hindquarter engagement):
        - Trot uphill x 5 reps
        - Canter uphill x 3 reps
    - Flat straight line poles:
        - Trot through 4–5 poles × 10 passes
    - Rein-back + transition combo:
        - Rein-back → trot → walk → halt → trot (1/4 markers on 20m circle) x 5 reps each rein

- Cool-down (10 mins):
    - Long and low trot and walk

EXERCISE PRESCRIPTION PRINCIPLES

Power prescription

Powerful movements can only be completed a few times consecutively before fatigue occurs. Training involves completing a small number of high intensity repetitions followed by a period of a least two minutes rest to allow for full recovery, before undertaking additional sets. There must be an excellent base of muscular strength before power should be trained.

A horse commencing power training may start with one set of 3-5 repetitions of a power exercise. As the horse adapts to the exercise, you may increase the prescription to 3-5 sets of 3-5 reps. The exercise is progressed by increasing the intensity of the exercise, not the number of repetitions or duration. For example, to progress a jumping grid activity, you would not jump the grid more times. Instead you might increase the height of one of the fences or the difficulty of the grid.

Exercises to train power can include gymnastic jumping/grids, jump outs and explosive upwards transitions, such as collected trot to extended trot.

EXERCISE PRESCRIPTION PRINCIPLES

Sample Training Session – Power Focus

Goal: Improve the horse's hindquarter power to consistently clear 1.10m courses without faults due to knockdowns, within 6 weeks.

- Warm-up (20 mins)
    - Active walk and trot with regular transitions between paces
    - Canter–walk–canter–walk transitions

- Main Set
    - Uphill canter sprints:
        - 10 sec uphill canter x 4 reps
        - Walk back downhill (3 minutes) until heart rate and breathing is recovered close to normal
    - Gymnastic jumping or bounce work:
        - Bounce grid x 3 rounds (low height, focus on form)
        - Rest period of 3 minutes between each round
    - Quick Transitions:
        - Trot–halt–canter–halt–trot x 5 sequences

- Cool-down
    - Walk on long rein for 8 minutes

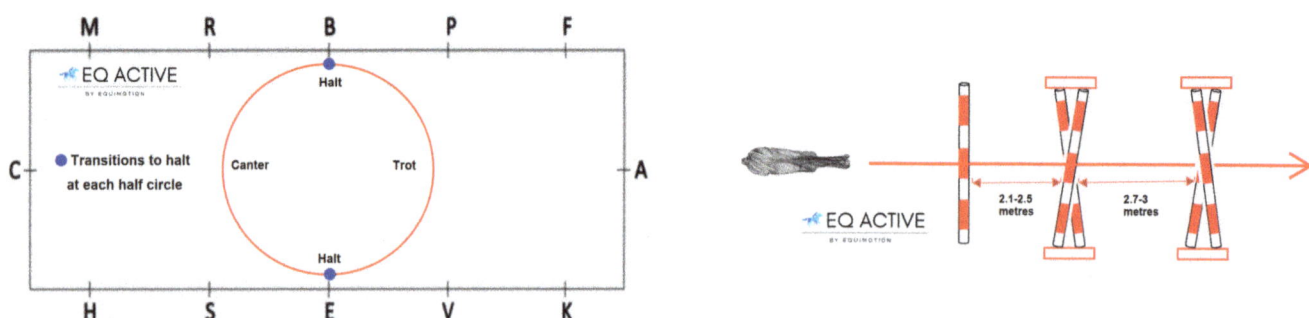

Examples of the set-up of the transition exercise between trot-halt-canter-halt-trot (left) and a simple bounce grid (right).

EXERCISE PRESCRIPTION PRINCIPLES

Flexibility prescription

Static stretches are often performed to improve range of movement of the body. Other techniques to improve flexibility include dynamic stretches and strengthening through range.

Static stretching

Static stretching is used to improve joint range of motion and flexibility. It involves reaching a certain range of motion or until a stretch sensation is felt and holding the position for a prescribed length of time.

Most of what we know about how long and often to perform stretching comes from the human literature. It's been found that, on average, performing stretching at least five days a week for a minimum of five minutes per session is required to promote range of motion improvements.

While the literature in horses is limited, there has been one study that found performing two repetitions, one for a 10 second hold and the other for 20 seconds, three times per week led to an increase in joint range of motion in the stifle, hock and shoulder.

Most people limit a stretch to the point of strong sensation, stopping short of pain. This can be difficult to determine in a horse, and you must use your judgement as to the range to take the stretch into. Initially it's better to be cautious and go slowly until the horse is accustomed to the exercise. A horse showing signs of discomfort, such as attempting to pull the limb away, may be a sign that the stretch sensation is too much, and a smaller range should be applied.

Strength training to improve range of motion

Some research has found that there is no significant difference between strength training and static stretching on improving range of motion in people. While this is yet to be studied in horses, (and there are still some gaps in the human literature), it suggests that if flexibility gains are desired, using either strength training or stretching can have positive effects.

Examples of strength training through range in the horse can include poles, turns and circles, lateral movements and inclines. You can apply the same prescription principles as you do for strength training. The bonus here is that you get two benefits – improved strength and flexibility – in one!

EXERCISE PRESCRIPTION PRINCIPLES

Dynamic stretching/mobility

Dynamic stretching involves performing a controlled movement through the range of motion of the active joint/s. Dynamic mobilisation exercises (DMEs) are a good example of this type of mobility exercise. Other examples include lateral and bending exercises in hand or under saddle.

Dynamic stretching or mobility exercises should be performed as short, controlled sets of repeated movements that prepare the body for exercise. It is low intensity exercise, and may commonly be part of a warm-up. In most cases, completing 5-10 minutes of dynamic stretching as part of your warm-up is appropriate. This might include a number of different exercises such as dynamic mobilisation exercises (DMEs), bending exercises, such as tight turns or weaving, and lateral work in-hand or under saddle. Each exercise can be performed for 6-10 repetitions of 1-2 sets. The aim is to start with a smaller range and slower tempo, gradually increasing the range and speed to match the demands of the upcoming work. Exercises should flow with minimal rest between them. Progression can be achieved by increasing the range of motion you ask the horse to move into, and adding complexity, such as making turns tighter in a weaving exercise.

> **Sample Training Session – Flexibility Focus**
>
> **Goal:** Over the next 12 weeks, restore spinal flexion and hindlimb mobility in a 10-year-old gelding with a history of back pain, so he can maintain a soft, round frame at the walk and trot for 10 consecutive minutes under saddle, demonstrated in two consecutive training sessions by week 12.
>
> - Long-lining in walk
>   - large loops through 6 cones x 8 reps each direction
>   - serpentine x 3 each direction
>   - walk-halt-walk at ¼ markers on 20m circle x 6 each direction
>   - walk over 4 x straight line flat poles x 8 each direction
> - DMES
>   - chin between fetlocks 2 x 8 reps
>   - chin to hind fetlocks (left and right) 2 x 8 reps each direction
> - Hindlimb mobility
>   - Protraction stretch 30 sec hold x 2
>   - Retraction stretch 30 sec hold x 2

EXERCISE PRESCRIPTION PRINCIPLES

Prescribing exercise load in practice

Once you have determined what type of fitness you would like to train (aerobic, strength, power, endurance, mobility) and have chosen the exercises you will use, it is time to set your exercise prescription using the FITTP principles – ie repetitions, sets, duration of exercise and rest periods.

It is essential that you practice your prescription with your horse. As you practice the exercise, you will be assessing the horse's baseline fitness, strength and mobility. It is important to note how the horse is managing the prescription – is it too easy, too hard, or just right?

Say, for example, you want to do poles exercises with your horse. Rather than just do the same number of reps and sets you see people do on the internet or at your barn, practice it with your horse, assessing how many reps and sets they can do before they show signs of fatigue or poor technique.

Doing this can help you decide whether you need to make any modifications, such as:

- Lowering or increasing the pole height, reducing or increasing the number of poles, modifying the distance, or even choosing a different exercise.
- Reducing or increasing the number of reps and sets to ensure you achieve the desired effect of the exercise.

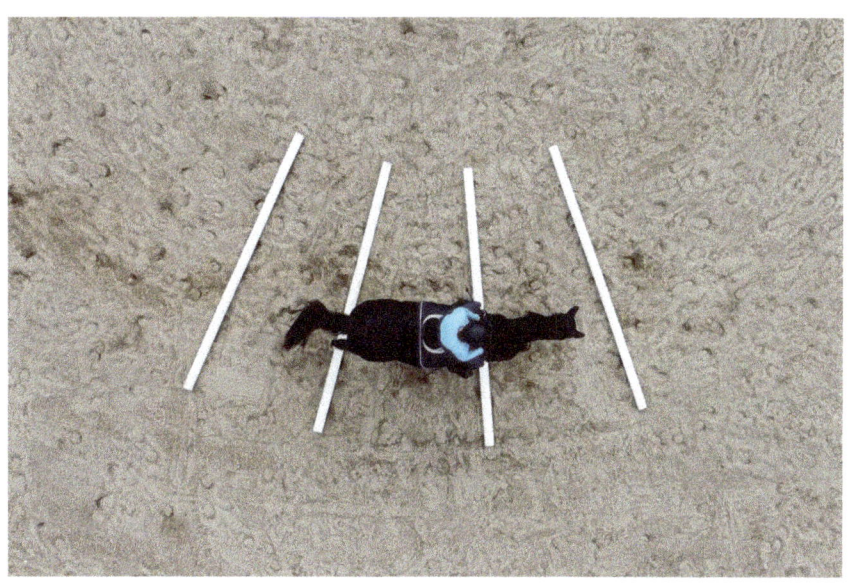

SETTING SMART GOALS

Goal setting is essential when designing a training program. It will help to make your training targeted and more effective. SMART goal setting can be a good way to do this. The following format is typically used:

Specific

The first step is making sure that the goal is specific. Consider the what, when, where and why, avoiding vague descriptions.

For example, a goal that states "*improve horse's strength*" is not at all specific.

However, a goal that states:

"*improve the horse's ability to perform the collected canter movements required in an Advanced test by increasing the strength of the hindquarter and trunk muscles*" is a much more specific goal and sets out clearly what needs to be done and why.

Measurable

A goal needs to be measurable so that you know if the goal has been achieved. Where possible, it's helpful to use objective measures.

An example of ensuring a goal is measurable would be to include detail such as:

"*perform 10 minutes of trot on a treadmill at a 4 degree incline at a speed of 14km/h.*"

"*perform 6 repetitions walking over 4 poles flat on the ground in a straight line without tripping or knocking the poles.*"

Achievable

A goal needs to be challenging, but it also needs to be achievable. It's important to not set yourself up to fail by setting a goal that is out of reach!

The goal needs to be realistic in relation to not only the horse's ability, age and fitness, but also your time, skill level, support network (e.g., trainer/coach) and resource availability. For example, for a newly purchased horse aged 15 and trained to novice dressage, setting a goal for that horse to be competing at Grand Prix in the next 2 years is not realistic.

SETTING SMART GOALS

Relevant

A goal needs to be meaningful to you and focus on achieving outcomes that you are focused on. It should answer the question *"does this goal matter to me or my larger aspirations?"*

For example, if your long term goal is to improve your horse's endurance to enable you to compete in long-format endurance events, a relevant short-term goal might be *"increase the duration of daily training rides to 3 hours"*. This goal is relevant because it directly supports the aim of improving endurance for competition.

A goal that states *"improve collected trot"* would be less relevant in this context as it doesn't contribute to the long-term goal.

Time-bound

Avoid vague timeframes and aim to be as specific as possible, while also being flexible in modifying deadlines when setbacks may occur.

Making the above goal time-bound would involve stating:

"increase the duration of daily training rides to 3 hours by x date"

Other important considerations to make in the goal setting process involve:

- Consider your long-term goal and break it down into smaller short-term goals that will help achieve the long-term goal. Ticking off these short-term goals can be motivating and help you see the path to success.

- Record your progress. The path to success is rarely linear, and sometimes it will not be possible to achieve all the goals within the set timeframe. When these (inevitable!) setbacks occur, it can be helpful to look back and see that overall you have made progress from where you started.

STRAIGHTNESS & SYMMETRY

Assessing symmetry and straightness in your horse

As horse owners and riders, we work towards our horse being as symmetrical and straight as possible so that they can move efficiently and perform to the best of their ability, whilst lowering the risk of developing injury. It's important to regularly look at your horse to recognise asymmetry, so that you can address this with appropriate training. Whilst mild asymmetry is very normal, we can improve on moderate to significant functional asymmetries to promote long term physical well-being, soundness and performance.

Consider the following factors:
- Is there even muscle development on the equivalent body parts left and right?
- Is there muscle balance from the front to the back end – is your horse very muscular through the neck and shoulders, but lacking in the hindquarters? This may indicate that your horse is 'front wheel drive' and overusing the front end to pull themselves along, rather than pushing with their hindquarters.
- Does the muscle balance look even from the topline compared to the underside of the body?
- Does your horse travel better on one rein (direction) compared to the other?
- Do they bend equally (and easily) in both directions?
- Do their hindlimbs track into the forelimbs when travelling in a straight line, or are they on three tracks? Is there a straight line through the body from the poll through the neck and spine to the tail?
- Do the shoulders or hindquarters fall in or out on the circle – and if so, in which direction does this occur? Is there an even curve through the horse's body from head to tail that matches the shape of the circle?
- Are your horse's ears level / does their nose tip to one side?
- Is your horse able to keep a steady rhythm during all activities? If your horse rushes, or alternatively loses forward momentum, it may be a sign they are crooked or unbalanced.
- Do they perform lateral work equally in both directions?
- Is your rein contact equal in all situations (when travelling straight and on circles, and when applying aids)?
- Do you as the rider feel even weight in your seat bones and stirrups (this assumes that you are symmetrical!)?
- Does your horse feel like they push equally with both hindlimbs (consider different situations, for example, you might only feel an uneven push with a lengthened trot)?
- Are the steps equal with each pair of limbs or does one limb have less height on the swing or step not as far forward?
- Does your horse have better canter quality on one lead?
- Is there a preferred lead your horse lands on following a jump?
- Does your saddle regularly slip to one side?

STRAIGHTNESS & SYMMETRY

Training symmetry and straightness

There are many simple ways that we can improve our horse's symmetry and straightness in daily management and training. Here are some ideas to try:

- Complete tasks from both sides of the horse – train your horse to lead from both sides, and mount and dismount from both sides of the horse (this is a great challenge to improve the rider's symmetry too!)
- Dismount to take away the influence of the tack and rider, and train groundwork. This is a wonderful way to develop your horse physically, as well as improve their response to aids. It can also strengthen the relationship with your horse. Some exercises that you can try include variations of turning (weaves, circles, serpentines), turn about the haunches, turn about the forehand, leg yielding in hand (across the arena and along the long side), side pass, and negotiating poles in hand. We share some examples in the case study below.
- Teach your horse to long line or drive. This is a great way to view and train your horse's straightness and way of travelling from behind.
- Gymnastic exercises – there are many coaches and resources available for straightness and gymnastic training. Find one that works best for you and your horse.
- Train both sides and direction of travel evenly. There are apps available that measure the amount of time spent training in each direction, or simply use a stopwatch.
- Rider symmetry assessment and training – it is crucial that riders ensure they are physically conditioned for riding and address any obvious asymmetry in themselves. There is research that shows asymmetry in riders can lead to the development of movement abnormalities including lameness in the horse. We discuss this further in Chapter 7.
- Monitor for signs of lameness such as head nod or hip drop, as well as pain behaviours (see Chapter 4 for further information) and seek veterinary assessment if anything is observed.

Investing time to improve your horse's symmetry, straightness and posture will allow the development of a supple, strong and robust horse.

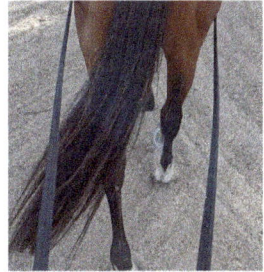 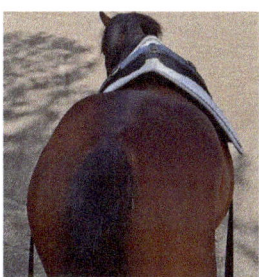 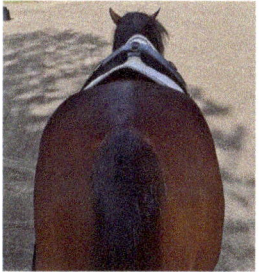 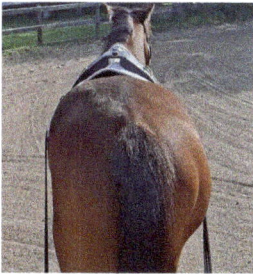

Long lining is a great way to assess foot placement, body alignment, and symmetry of side to side swing of the ribcage and hindquarters left to right. You can see in this series of images that this horse has greater bend to the left compared to the right.

STRAIGHTNESS & SYMMETRY

Case Study

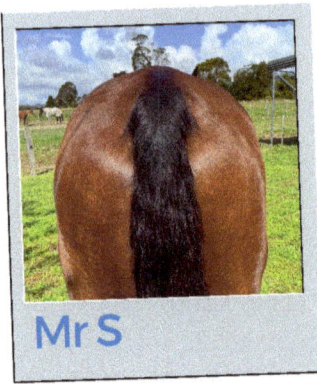

Mr S

- 5 year old Warmblood gelding.
- Mr S was bred by his owner to compete in eventing and showjumping.
- Owner was concerned about his crookedness and difficulty in building up muscle in the right hindquarter.

Mr S's owner started to notice he was having some difficulty travelling to the right rein. When competing, he was scoring less for right direction activities in his dressage tests. The owner reported that the right canter lead was more difficult to maintain. He would shift his hindquarters to the right when backing up, or pushing up a hill, and they noticed he wasn't building up muscle on the right hind like the left. There was some concern that there was a niggling, chronic lameness because of this. He would often be difficult to ride straight, feeling like a wiggly worm and tending to travel on the forehand.

In order to exclude a clinical lameness as the cause of his movement difficulties, Mr S had a full veterinary lameness work up. He was determined sound and pain-free by the vet. The next step for the owner was to work with a physio to implement a training program to address his hindquarter asymmetry, as well as strength and proprioception deficits.

The following exercises were included:

- Proprioception exercises.
- Hindquarter and whole body postural strength exercises – to teach Mr S how to hold his body in a better posture, as well as activating the right hindquarter stability muscles.
- Groundwork exercises – to take away the influence and additional challenge of the rider and to improve the symmetry of the right and left sides of his body. Examples were lateral and turning exercises in each direction.
- Pole exercises – to improve the awareness of where his body is in space and encourage him to place his hind feet differently. Examples were walking beside or between poles, adding transitions to halt as well as rein back alongside the poles. He found this incredibly difficult to start!

STRAIGHTNESS & SYMMETRY

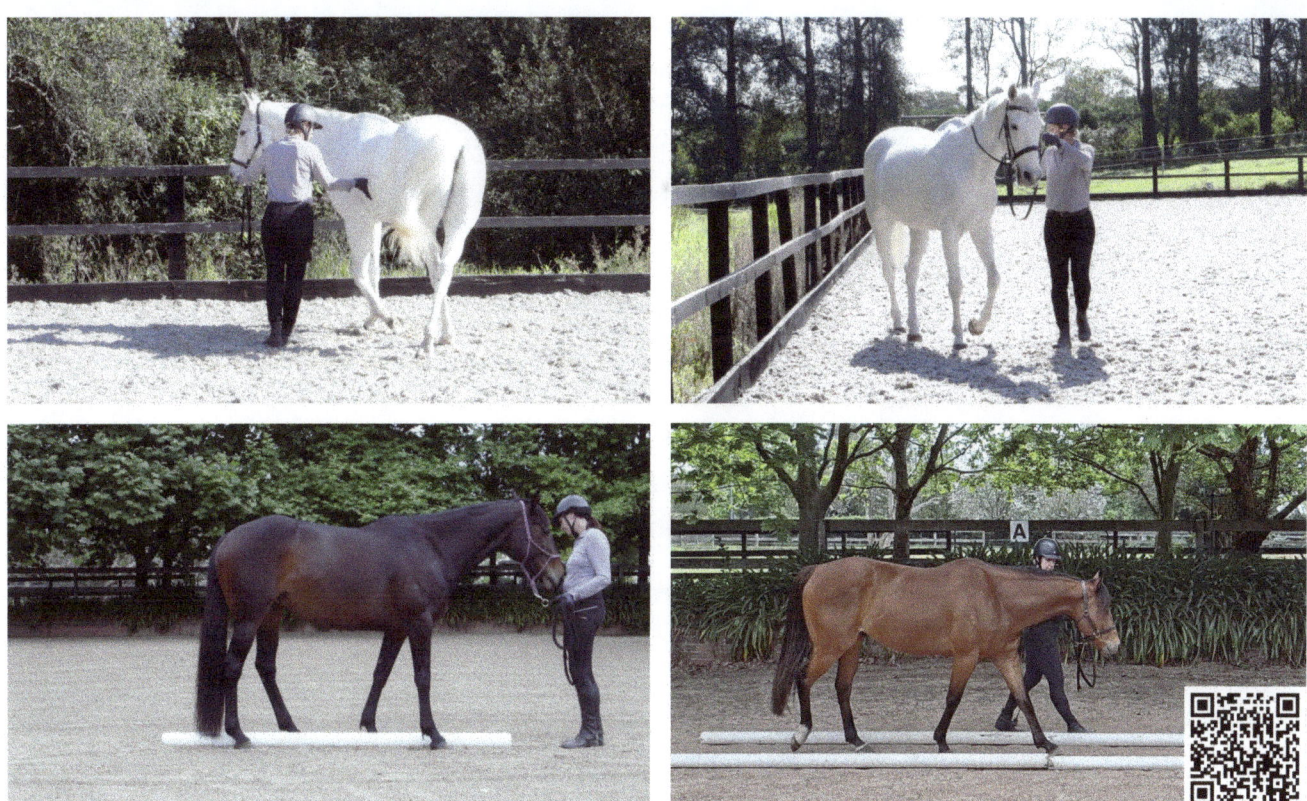

Examples of groundwork exercises performed - tight turn with rib pressure, leg yield in hand, , straddling a pole and back in-hand between 2 poles.

6 weeks after introducing the exercises to his training, Mr S was much better in trot on a straight line – there was less side to side rotation of the pelvis and the rider reported it was easier to keep him straight under saddle.

SKILL DEVELOPMENT

When introducing a new skill, particularly a high-level movement, the most effective approach is to break the skill down into smaller stages. Each stage should be practised and consolidated before moving on to the next, allowing the horse to build the strength, mobility, fitness, and proprioception required to perform the complete skill confidently and safely. As the horse progresses, the separate stages can be combined to build the full, more complex skill.

It's also important to ensure that the horse can perform the skill consistently, even when under pressure (such as at a competition or when fatigued). Throughout the process, training should be adapted to the horse's individual needs, considering their current strength, mobility, fitness and coordination. Allowing time for rest and recovery is crucial. By following this step-by-step approach, new skills can be introduced in a way that is progressive and safe, giving the horse a better chance at successfully learning new skills without injuring themselves.

Case Study

Ms K

- 11 year old Warmblood mare.
- Owner wants to start training canter pirouettes, with the goal of moving up to Small Tour in 18 months. Ms K has a past history of hindlimb suspensory injury and her owner wants to avoid re-injury.

Breaking down the canter pirouette

One of the most advanced dressage movements, the canter pirouette requires exceptional collection and strength. The canter becomes almost on the spot, with the inside hind leg acting as a pivot. The hindlimb joints show marked flexion, lifting clearly off the ground and placing back down nearly in the same spot, creating a small circle around the pivot.

The shoulders rotate around the hindquarters in a larger arc, with the outside forelimb crossing over the inside. The movement should remain balanced, without tilting or uneven weight in the shoulders. Throughout, the horse maintains a consistent three-beat, slow, yet cadenced, rhythm.

SKILL DEVELOPMENT

Key components required for this movement include:
- A collected canter.
- Lowering of the hindquarters – increased flexion of all the joints and increased weight-bearing of the hindlimbs.
- Marked elevation of the forehand.
- Lateral bend in the direction of travel, with the haunches positioned inward.
- Forelimbs describing a larger circle around the more grounded hindlimbs.

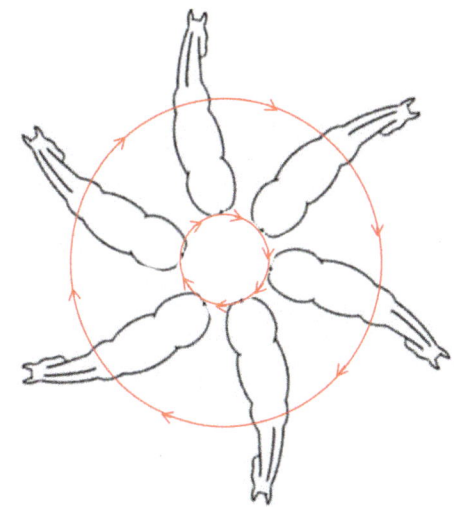

Which exercises were performed and why

1. Transitions
Walk–canter–walk and halt–rein back–canter transitions focus both on control (downward transitions) and propulsion (upwards transitions). They also strengthen muscles that allow the horse to raise the forehand and lower the hindquarters, a key element of a canter pirouette. For strength and skill development, Ms K performed 3–5 repetitions per exercise, repeated across 3–4 sets, with short walk breaks between sets to allow for recovery.

2. Collected canter
This is key, as the horse must have strength and control in collected canter before being able to perform the pirouette. The emphasis should be on maintaining quality and rhythm of the canter. Ms K performed 20-30 seconds of collected canter on a 15m circle, performing 4-5 sets per training session. Between each set she had a rest period of 1-2 minutes, moving between working canter, walk and trot large around the arena.

3. Travers
This is a great exercise to help prepare the body for the canter pirouette as it helps to create the posture and body position required (i.e., bend through the body towards the direction of travel). The owner focused on ensuring Ms K could master this at slower speeds in walk and trot before she commenced the exercise in canter, particularly on the circle.

SKILL DEVELOPMENT

Ms K's owner progressed the travers exercise in the following ways:
- Starting in walk first, before progressing to trot and canter.
- Performing on a straight line first, then progressed to performing on a circle.
- Varying the tempo from collected to medium paces.
- Moving to a working pirouette – performing travers down the leg side, then adding a circle (starting as large as needed to), maintaining the travers position on circle.
- Making sure Ms K was comfortably established with easier exercises before moving onto the more challenging exercises. This means that she was able to maintain the posture required without resistance, maintain rhythm of the canter beats, perform the exercise the same on both reins (symmetry) and coordinate the movement smoothly.

Examples of the exercises performed (from left to right): travers in walk along the long side, travers in walk on a circle

How to perform travers / hindquarters in on a circle

- Start with a 20 metre circle and make this smaller as able.
- Make sure body position, tempo and footfalls are correct and manageable. Progress to smaller circles only when you can achieve all of this at the current level you are training.
- Four to six strides of quarters in should be followed by either straightness or by enlarging the circle ('active rest time'). Complete 2-4 sets (this prescription adheres to strength training principles).

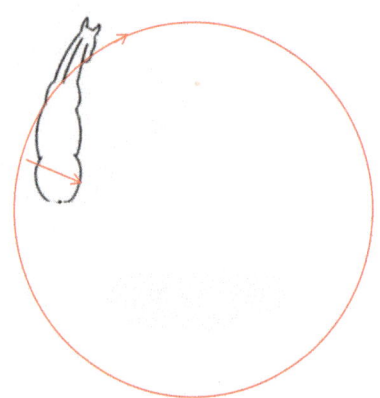

SKILL DEVELOPMENT

4. Variations of the working pirouette

The final exercise was to start with ¼ turns, and then build up from there as Ms K became stronger and more coordinated with performing the exercise. One example is to ride a square with four ¼ pirouettes in each corner.

Ms K was asked to perform this exercise by:
- Riding in a "square" shape with the hindquarters positioned in.
- At every corner of the square, ride a ¼ pirouette (90° turn).
- This was performed initially at walk, then progressed to collected canter, performing 2-3 sets of 4 reps.

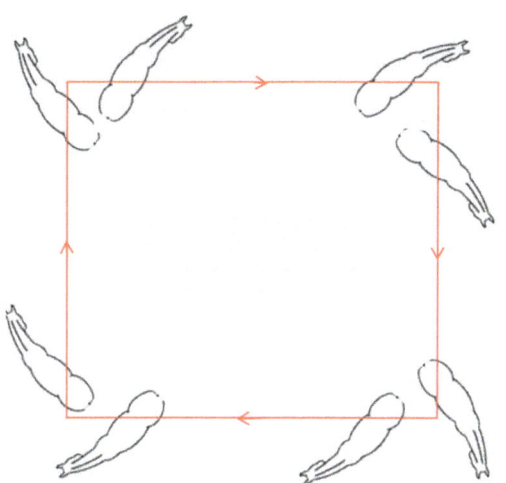

Signs to alter exercises or seek veterinary advice

It's important to monitor every horse for signs of lameness or discomfort which might suggest they're not coping with their workload, no matter what stage of training they're at.

Particular signs Ms K's owner was monitoring during her program included:
- Fatigue or a reluctance to start or continue work.
- Inability to maintain rhythm or losing the correct footfalls.
- Falling out of pace and/or refusing to move forward.
- Losing posture, for example raising the head or hollowing through the body.
- A change in the rein contact, occurring consistently or repeatedly.
- Tripping or stumbling.
- Pain signs, particularly those in the Ridden Horse Pain Ethogram (see Chapter 4 for more detail on monitoring pain).

Chapter 3
LOAD MANAGEMENT
The relationship between load and risk of injury

LOAD MANAGEMENT

What does "load" mean?

Load refers to the physical stresses that affect a horse's body such as movement, the amount of force through the limbs when they hit the ground with each stride or changes in temperature. These stresses can be external from the environment, like uneven footing or a wet surface, or internal, such as the strain from muscle contractions during exercise.

Bone, muscle, ligament, and tendon all adapt in response to load. These tissues remain healthy and function optimally when they experience the right balance of load, including how much load is placed on them, and how often that occurs. Understanding how these loads influence the body is crucial, especially when designing a training program. By carefully managing how these forces are applied – through things such as exercise, hoof care and recovery strategies – we can help lower the risk of injury.

However, this balance of load is not universal. Each horse will respond uniquely to different levels of load based on factors such as genetics, training history, and overall health. Additionally, different tissues have varying sensitivities to load; for instance, bone is particularly influenced by the size of the load rather than how often it's applied.

What we can follow as a general rule is that progressive, controlled loading* helps improve strength and soft tissue adaptation. Overloading (i.e., doing too much, too soon) can lead to potential tissue damage, such as a tendon or muscular strain injury. Conversely, underloading (not doing enough) can result in reduced muscular size and strength, reduced tendon elasticity and increased injury risk.

> *__Progressive Controlled Loading__ means gradually increasing exercise demands to help the horse build strength and reduce injury risk. For example, if you're training a horse for eventing, you wouldn't start straight away with a full cross-country course. You might begin with short canter sets on flat ground, then slowly increase the duration, add in gentle hills and introduce small jumps. Over time, you'd build up the intensity by making the sessions longer, adding bursts of speed, using varied terrain, and raising jump height (adding one variable at a time). This step-by-step approach helps to strengthen soft tissues, bone and the cardiovascular system without overloading them too quickly. Skipping steps or doing too much, too soon is a common cause of injury. Progressive controlled loading will help to avoid that.

LOAD MANAGEMENT

Why do we need to measure load?

We measure load in horses so that we can structure training programs that will be safe and effective. Measuring load allows us to quantify how much stress is being placed on the horse's body during exercise. The right amount of load stimulates bones and soft tissues to adapt and strengthen, while too little can lead to de-conditioning and increased risk of injury.

Measuring load is especially important when we consider the anatomy of the horse's limbs. The lower limb is unique, designed for speed, efficiency and shock absorption. Unlike humans, a horse's lower leg contains no muscle. It is composed primarily of bone, tendons and ligaments.

The suspensory apparatus

The suspensory apparatus is one of the most important features of the horse's lower leg for stability and performance. It is made up of the suspensory ligament, the sesamoid bones and the distal sesamoidean ligaments. The primary role of the suspensory apparatus is to prevent the fetlock from moving into excessive extension, or "drop" towards the ground. It acts almost like a sling underneath the fetlock to help control the amount of range the joint moves through. It plays a vital role in supporting and stabilising the fetlock, but because of this, it is highly prone to injury. Suspensory ligament injury in the hindlimbs is a common problem in dressage horses.

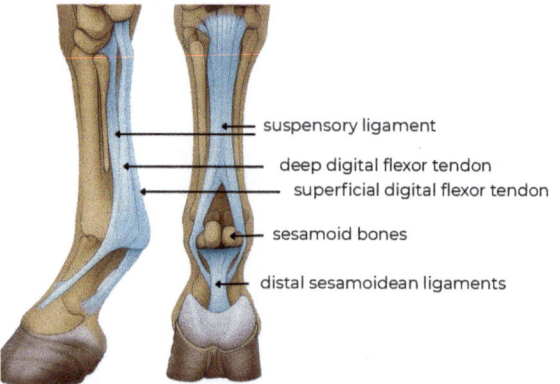

The flexor tendons

There are two flexor tendons that run down the back of each limb, the superficial digital flexor tendon (SDFT) and the deep digital flexor tendon (DDFT). These tendons are essential for efficient movement and shock absorption. The tendons act like a spring, storing and releasing energy to propel the horse forward. This efficiency reduces muscular effort in the upper limb, especially at high speeds and when jumping.

LOAD MANAGEMENT

They also function to flex the fetlock, pastern and coffin joints. The DDFT attaches within the hoof on the coffin bone, and plays a key role in providing stability of the hoof when it's in contact with the ground. Like the suspensory ligament, the flexor tendons do provide some support to the fetlock, but their primary role is locomotion and shock absorption.

Much like the suspensory apparatus, their function makes them highly susceptible to injury. At high speeds and during impact on landing a jump, tendons stretch close to their physiological limit. Repetitive high loads can cause microdamage, leading to injury if rest and recovery aren't prioritised. Flexor tendon injuries are common, especially in the SDFT of the forelimbs. They carry high re-injury rates (40–60%). Racehorses, eventers and showjumpers are typically most affected.

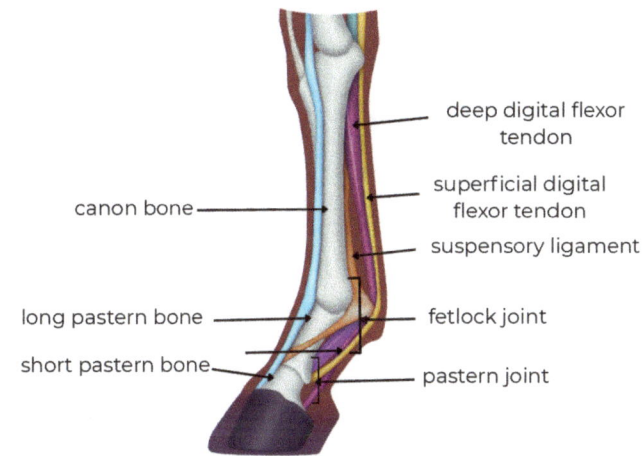

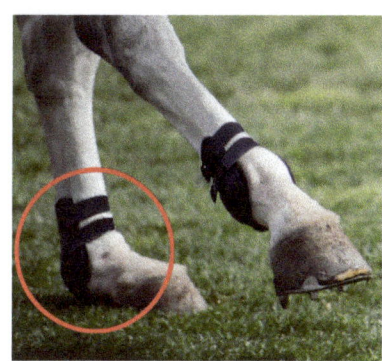

An example of fetlock hyperextension or "drop", which places extra load on the suspensory apparatus and flexor tendons.

Normal tissue response to training load

Bone, muscle, ligament and tendon all constantly adapt to the loads placed on them. When exposed to the right balance of frequency and amount of load, these structures will typically stay strong and healthy.

Bones respond to how much load is placed on them, with higher amounts stimulating bone remodelling and improved bone density. Insufficient load, such as occurs during periods of box rest, can lead to loss of bone density. Muscles respond to both how often and how hard they work, developing greater strength, endurance and power with regular use. Under-loading leads to muscle atrophy (loss of muscle bulk), which can place more strain on surrounding joints and other soft tissues. Tendons and ligaments typically adapt more slowly, gradually becoming stronger and more resilient when exposed to regular, controlled loading.

OVERUSE INJURY

Muscle, tendon, ligament, and bone injuries are common in performance and racehorses. While it's impossible to avoid all injury, there are steps you can take to help reduce the risk, starting with a clear understanding of why and how injuries occur.

Types of injuries

Musculoskeletal injuries (injuries to bone or soft tissues such as muscle, tendon or ligaments) typically fall into two broad categories. The first is an acute or traumatic injury, which occurs when the force on the structure surpasses its tolerance at that moment in time. This can happen if a horse is pushed beyond its physical limits, as the result of an accident (such as a fall) or due to inadequate preparation for the demands of a particular activity. An extreme example is taking an unfit, out of work horse out to perform a high intensity three-day event.

Acute or traumatic injuries are actually less common than people may think. While in many cases it may seem like your horse suddenly came out of the paddock sore or randomly pulled up lame after a training session, the more common cause of many musculoskeletal injuries is related to overuse.

What is an overuse injury and why do they occur?

An overuse injury occurs when tissue is damaged due to repetitive demands placed on it over time. Issues with training or load management is the main reason that they occur.

This includes:
- Inconsistent training.
- Insufficient rest periods within a training session e.g., cantering for 15 minutes despite the horse showing signs of fatigue such as a loss of posture or tripping.
- Insufficient rest periods between sessions, such as completing two or three high intensity training sessions back-to-back before the horse has fully recovered.
- Spending too much time doing one particular movement or activity, in one direction or on one type of surface.
- Inadequate warm-up and cool-down practices.
- Repetitive high-impact forces, such as jumping big fences multiple times in a week, or galloping more than two or three sessions per week.

OVERUSE INJURY

Some horses can be more prone to developing an overuse injury than others due to biomechanical disadvantages, such as:
- poor conformation
- previous injury
- hypermobility (excessive joint range of motion)
- poor gait / movement patterns
- poor posture

What happens to the tissues in an overuse injury?

The right amount of exercise stimulates bones and soft tissues to adapt, building strength and resilience. However, if the training load is too heavy, too frequent or increases too quickly, the tissues can't keep up. Rather than build strength, they suffer fatigue and become damaged, leading to injury.

- **Bone:** the most common overuse injuries to affect bone are stress fractures. These result from repetitive high loads during activities such as racing and eventing. The bone develops microdamage that outpaces the bone's ability to repair itself, resulting in small cracks in the bone. Common sites are in the limbs and pelvis.
- **Muscle:** muscle can also develop microdamage, leading to soreness and inflammation. In more severe cases, excessive load can result in muscular strains or tears (an acute on top of overuse injury). Muscles that are weak and less developed are more prone to developing an overuse injury.
- **Tendon and ligaments:** these are the most common structures in the horse to suffer from an overuse injury. Repeated overload causes tiny tears, inflammation and/or thickening that reduces structural integrity and tendon elasticity, increasing the risk of full or partial tears.

Working to put in place good training practices will go a long way in reducing the risk of overuse injury. To do this it's important to consider two basic principles: The Goldilocks Principle and Progressive Overload .

THE GOLDILOCKS PRINCIPLE

When we think about the story of Goldilocks and the Three Bears, Goldilocks wanted the chair, the bed and the porridge to be just right. In the same way, our training loads need to be just right. This means ensuring they are high enough to cause adaptation of the bones and soft tissues, but not so high as to cause or exacerbate injury.

When we apply this principle to people, we advise that after an exercise session you should feel you've worked hard but you recover within 24-48 hours (JUST RIGHT). Soreness that lasts longer than 48 hours suggests you need to back off a little (TOO HOT), while no soreness or feeling of effort suggests you need to push a little more (TOO COLD). However, when our horses can't tell us if they are sore or not following exercise, how do we know if what we are doing is "just right"?

We know that in a horse's regular training, we need to train at a consistent level that increases gradually in order to see improvement. Sometimes we will have larger increases in training load (such as during competition or clinics) and sometimes we will have decreases (light work days or holidays/spelling). The horse's body can cope with these well, as long as we have a consistent level of training the remainder of the time.

Determining "just right" loads in the horse

Signs the horse may not be working hard enough will simply be that you are seeing little to no change in their performance, muscle development or movement (NO CHANGE = TOO COLD).

Signs that they may be doing too much can be increased resistance to training, behavioural changes, facial or body pain markers, lameness or poor performance (NEGATIVE CHANGE = TOO HOT). It's important to note that sometimes no or negative change will occur if there is an underlying issue and a veterinary opinion should always be sought.

If the horse is gaining or maintaining muscle and condition, is moving well, can handle more challenging work and appears happy and willing, chances are you're getting the loads "just right" (POSITIVE CHANGE = JUST RIGHT).

Use of objective measures to ensure the load is "just right"

In order to take the guesswork out of determining if the load is "just right", objective outcome measures should be used wherever possible. An objective outcome measure is a measurable test repeated at regular intervals to make sure that the horse is progressing. Examples are discussed in more detail later in Chapter 4. Regular measurements are essential to determine that the horse stays on the right path.

PROGRESSIVE OVERLOAD

The progressive overload principles states that the body must be progressively loaded in order to gain increases in strength, power or endurance. A single exercise session leads to fatigue and mild cellular damage within bone and soft tissues, which results in short-term adaptive responses. This exercise stimulus triggers the tissues to repair and grow stronger.

When exercise is performed regularly and the training stimulus is increased gradually, the adaptation that occurs during the recovery period leads to an overall improvement in performance. Therefore, the basis of any training program is to continually provide increased levels of training stress to improve performance. Training stress should be increased gradually and progressively to continue building strength. Raising it too quickly can lead to injury. It's important to remember that the body can only adapt so far – there is a limit to how much stress the body can be placed under.

Stress / load
⌄⌄
Damage
⌄⌄
Rest / recovery
⌄⌄
Adaption / growth

Each individual horse will differ in relation to how well they can cope with this stress. When training is too vigorous and/or rest periods between training sessions are too short, performance is reduced because of an imbalance between training stress and recovery.

> *Rest is an integral part of progressive overload.* Recovery time and strategies are equally important to schedule in a program as load.

REST AND RECOVERY

Considering rest and recovery

While the training load may be "just right", if the rest/recovery time is too short, negative changes to bone and soft tissues may occur. Measurement of muscle enzymes and free radicals within muscles after exercise can help us understand how well the exercise training will stimulate improvements in fitness. Studies in racehorses and long distance endurance horses showed that 24-72 hours of recovery were needed for horses to return to pre-exercise levels following strenuous activity. Untrained horses took longer to recover than those that were trained. These results are comparable to the human research and suggest that recovery periods of 24-72 hours are required between intense training sessions, especially if the horse is unaccustomed to that level of exercise. Giving your horse one to three days of rest or low intensity exercise following a very strenuous training or competition session will contribute to reducing the risk of injury and fatigue due to overtraining, by allowing the tissues to recover fully before the next training stimulus occurs.

Rest between sets

Rest between sets refers to the recovery period taken between blocks of an exercise during a workout. For example, you might complete three sets of two circles in collected trot during one training session. You would trot two circles, then rest for two minutes before repeating another two circles. A study in humans showed that they can gain muscular strength when rest periods between exercise sets are shorter than 60 seconds. However, to maximise strength gains, durations of greater than two minutes were required in individuals who were already performing strength training. In untrained individuals, short to moderate rest intervals of 60-120 seconds were sufficient for maximising muscular strength performance. While we don't currently have any research that has looked at this in horses, we can safely apply the same timeframes.

Ensure you allow for regular rest breaks during a training session that focuses on high intensity exercises designed to build your horse's strength, such as training collected movements or jumping.

Recovery days between training sessions

Many riders train their horses 6-7 days a week. It's important to consider how the type and intensity of training is structured across the week to avoid the risk of overtraining due to insufficient recovery between sessions. A recovery day doesn't have to mean complete rest, but could involve a low intensity session, such as a trail ride or ground work session.

REST AND RECOVERY

Researchers investigated in rats how muscles respond to resistance training and how rest intervals between sessions affect these responses, which included changes in cellular and molecular levels. They found that when there was a 48-hour recovery period, the muscle growth responses were much greater compared to shorter recovery periods of 8 or 24 hours. Other studies have found that in untrained young women, it takes over 72 hours to fully recover muscle strength after a resistance training session.

Recovery days between sessions allow muscles to adapt and prevent overtraining. Horses, like humans, may benefit from low-intensity recovery activities and sufficient time between intense sessions to optimise performance and reduce injury risk. After a demanding training day such as a challenging lesson, high-intensity fitness work or stepping up a level, consider allowing one to three days of rest (no work) or relative rest (low-intensity work such as hacking out). This gives both bone and soft tissues time to recover and supports optimal adaptation, helping build strength in response to the harder work.

Although each horse needs an individualised training and management plan, the following guidelines on how much recovery time is required following a training session can be applied. These are based on what we currently know from the research, and can be adjusted for each horse and their current training level.

- Low intensity session: 12 hours recovery time
- Medium intensity session: 12-24 hours recovery time
- Substantial intensity session: 24-48 hours recovery time
- High / extreme intensity session: 48-72 hours recovery time

Remember that what activity is low or high intensity will vary for each horse depending on their existing fitness level. It can be helpful to log your training sessions so that you keep track of the intensity of each session, allowing you to adjust your training days accordingly. We will discuss how to measure the intensity of a session in more detail later in this chapter.

REST AND RECOVERY

Practical recovery steps

- Allow your horse to cool down after a training session or at a competition. This includes at, a minimum, a period of walking. If the weather is warm or the horse has undergone a high-intensity session, additional methods such as cold water cooling with a hose or buckets is required. This helps regulate heart rate, breathing, and body temperature.
- Hydration is crucial. Research confirms that horses are most inclined to drink immediately after exercise, and allowing them to do so (even if they're still warm) is safe. Contrary to outdated myths, drinking at this time does not cause health issues like colic or laminitis. Denying access to water may lead to unnecessary sweating, electrolyte loss, and restlessness when confined to the stable while still warm. Horses drink about 25–30 litres of water a day in temperate climates, but in hot climates they should drink double that (60 litres). Use buckets to measure that your horse is drinking enough for their needs and the environment.
- Ensure your horse has somewhere comfortable and safe to lie down to sleep undisturbed.
- Allow access to roughage post-exercise. Electrolytes are essential for recovery and these occur naturally in roughage. In some cases, particularly if the intensity of exercise is high and temperatures hot, additional electrolyte supplement may be required. Speak to your vet regarding the products they recommend for your horse.
- Protein is a crucial component of musculoskeletal tissue, playing a pivotal role in muscle building and repair. It is important to ensure that your horse's diet includes high-quality protein. Researchers have examined the effects of feeding young horses rice bran oil and flaxseed oil, which contain omega-3 fatty acids, on inflammation and muscle damage after exercise. They found that including these oils in the horses' diet for 60 days reduced the increase in certain markers of inflammation and muscle damage, compared to horses not receiving the oils. Speak to your vet or nutritionist to help guide your horse's diet based on their individual needs.
- There is some research in humans, that shows consuming protein in the post-training period (1 hour or less) plays a potentially useful role in optimising physical performance and positively influencing the recovery process. Other studies have found that it is the quality of the protein, as opposed to the timing, that matters most. If you have the ability to, providing a high quality protein supplement immediately post-work may provide some benefit to your horse. As always, seek advice from your vet and or nutritionist for your individual horse.
- Preparing horses before competition is just as important as their post-event care. Ensuring that they are well-hydrated, have balanced electrolytes, and sufficient fitness for their discipline creates a strong foundation for recovery.

DETRAINING & RETURNING AFTER A SPELL

A lack of exercise (due to injury, spelling, adverse weather events or off-seasons) can lead to a decline in musculoskeletal and cardiorespiratory adaptations – reducing strength, endurance, and fitness.

During an 8-week spelling period, a previously high-level equine athlete will start to experience detraining effects on the body. Muscle mass and strength start to decline due to atrophy (muscle wasting), and bone remodelling slows, reducing bone density and increasing the risk of stress-related injuries if high-intensity training resumes too quickly.

Research shows that detraining in horses leads to a decline in aerobic capacity and metabolic efficiency, resulting in quicker fatigue when exercise is resumed. It has been found that even short periods of reduced training or stall rest decrease maximal oxygen consumption (VO_2max), cardiac output, and stroke volume in Thoroughbreds. While these changes are inevitable during rest, controlled movement (such as turnout or low-intensity exercise) can help mitigate these changes.

Turnout is important for horses during a spell, but doesn't compensate completely for the reduction in normal training load. Researchers in 2024 found that in a group of horses that had access to pasture turnout, those that maintained light exercise during a 12-week break had better topline muscling than those horses that had turnout only. No significant differences in fitness were observed between conditioned and non-conditioned horses, suggesting that while pasture access may help maintain some fitness during periods without ridden work, it is insufficient to preserve muscle mass.

If your horse's break from training has been longer than 2-3 weeks, it is essential to design a gradual and structured training program to bring them back into work. The longer the break, the more extended the return to work program should be. This will ensure that you safely rebuild strength, endurance and fitness, whilst minimising the risk of injury due to loading too quickly.

DETRAINING & RETURNING AFTER A SPELL

Case Study

- 13 year old Thoroughbred x Warmblood mare, competing 1* Eventing.
- Horse recently had a high intensity competition and training schedule before going on a 10-week spell due to owner's work and travel commitments.
- During the spelling period, Ms T was turned out 12 hours a day in a medium sized flat paddock, with horses either side in adjoining paddocks. Ms T is fairly quiet, and was observed mostly to walk around and graze during turnout.

Things the owner considered when the horse first came back into work:

- Nutrition – While Ms T was on a spell, the owner gradually adjusted her diet over several weeks, reducing high-energy feed and focusing on feeding roughage. She planned ahead to ensure that, as the horse returned to work, dietary changes were introduced gradually, rather than making sudden adjustments on the first day back. Higher energy feed was re-introduced slowly over the first 2-3 weeks of training.
- Saddle fit – It was noted that there was a slight change in Ms T's topline muscle when she first came back into work, so it was made a priority to get the saddle fitter out in the first week for a saddle fit. Some temporary adjustments with shims were made initially, with a plan to review the horse again in 4 weeks as her shape changed with an increase in workload.
- While Ms T's owner was keen to jump straight back into training, she noticed pretty quickly that Ms T seemed stiffer under saddle, and was finding circling in one direction and lateral movements more difficult than she had previously. Her general fitness was noted to have dropped. To re-introduce work, the following steps were taken:
    - Walk, walk and more walk in the first few weeks! Walk work can be incredibly valuable, especially in the early stages of returning to work after a spell or injury. It places low load on the limbs but still helps build muscular strength and control, especially when you combine it with walk-halt transitions, variations within the pace, lateral movements, circles, pole work, and even walking over different surfaces or gradients.

DETRAINING & RETURNING AFTER A SPELL

- Canter wasn't reintroduced for the first 5 weeks, instead only included in a training session once it was observed that Ms T had improved suppleness, and was no longer displaying any resistance to lateral work in walk and trot.
- Jumping was not reintroduced until Ms T was comfortably working in all three gaits with good suppleness and balance. Small cross poles and simple grids were used first, as these encourage rhythm, straightness, and strength without placing too high a load on the limbs. The focus was on keeping the effort low, with only a few repetitions in each session, gradually building height and technicality as Ms T's strength and fitness improved.
- Cross-country training was the final stage to be re-introduced. Initial sessions involved schooling over small fences. Longer gallops and more demanding efforts over larger obstacles were only added once Ms T had regained sufficient conditioning through flatwork, trot and canter sets, and low-intensity jumping. This gradual progression allowed her musculoskeletal system time to adapt to the increased impact and intensity of cross-country work, reducing the risk of overload or injury.

A break of 10 weeks typically means that it will take at least 10 weeks to bring a horse back into full fitness, if not more. Aerobic fitness is gained sooner than musculoskeletal changes, such as muscular strength. Some soft tissues, like tendon, can take even longer than 12-16 weeks to regain their pre-spell condition. This will vary from horse to horse, depending on individual factors such as the horse's level of fitness before the spell, their discipline and any history of injury. Pushing a horse to return to their previous level of training too quickly leads to a significantly increased risk of overloading the soft tissues, so it is essential to take a progressive, consistent approach.

DETRAINING & RETURNING AFTER A SPELL

Sample weekly training plan – week 1

Monday
1. Ridden Arena Session 30 min
   a. Rein back to walk on x 5
   b. Walk / halt transitions on a circle x 4 each direction
   c. Leg yield step ladder in walk x 4 each direction
   d. Walk serpentines x 3 each direction
   e. Shoulder in walk long side x 3 each direction
   f. Stretching frame walk 10 min

Tuesday
1. Long lining / poles session 20 min
   a. weave shallow loops long line x 6 each direction
   b. long lining 2 loops 2 x 3 each direction
   c. long lining straight lines, change of direction 10 min
   d. Snake poles x 4 each direction
   e. straight line poles alternate ends raised x 8

Wednesday
Rest

Thursday
1. Ridden Arena Session 30 min
   a. Rein back to walk on x 5
   b. Walk / halt transitions on a circle x 4 each direction
   c. Leg yield step ladder in walk x 4 each direction
   d. Walk serpentines x 3 each direction
   e. Shoulder in walk long side x 3 each direction
   f. Stretching frame walk 10 min

Friday
1. Hack out 45 minutes – mostly walk, small amounts of trot

Saturday
1. Long lining / poles session 20 min
   a. weave shallow loops long line x 6 each direction
   b. long lining 2 loops 2 x 3 each direction
   c. long lining straight lines, change of direction 10 min
   d. Snake poles x 4 each direction
   e. straight line poles alternate ends raised x 8

Sunday
Rest

MEASURING WORKLOAD

Workload is defined as how much work the tissues do during a period of time.

It can be measured in two ways:
- External workload – is the measurable physical demands of the exercise. This includes things you can track such as distance covered, time spent training, speed, and number of jumps or strides.
- Internal workload – refers to how the horse physiologically and subjectively responds to exercise. It is often assessed using heart rate, rate of perceived exertion, or biochemical markers.

Measuring external workload

Measuring external workload is relatively easy to do in the horse, and can be achieved using technology, observational methods and/or manual tracking. Examples include:
- **GPS data** – measuring distance, speed, acceleration and deceleration. There are a number of free apps you can download to do this (such as KER ClockIt Sport), or alternatively use the features on your phone or smartwatch. You can set a stop watch or timer to measure time spent working within a particular gait.
- **Stride Analysis** – measuring variables such as step frequency, stride length and symmetry (comparing time spent in each direction).
- **Training logs** – keeping a manual training log in which you record any number of variables, such as session duration, terrain type, and intensity. It can also be useful to record variables such as the number of jumps per session (including height and difficulty) and time spent in each gait and in each direction.

There are a number of apps available that allows you to easily record external workload during a training session. These include Equimetre (Arioneo), Seaver, EquiLab, KER ClockIt Sport and Equisense.

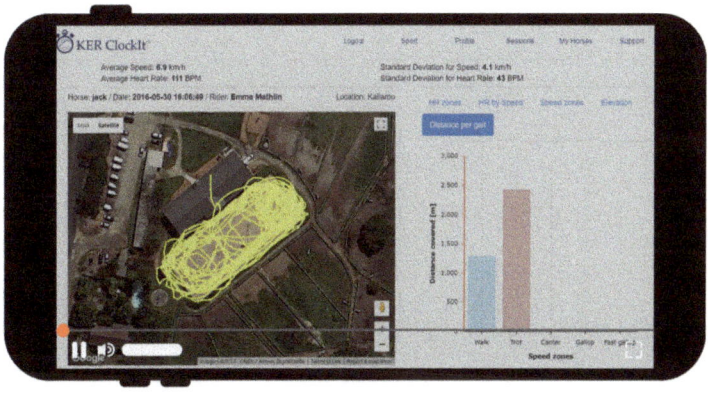

KER ClockIt Sport is one of several apps you can use to measure external workload. Some of them also connect to heart rate monitors to record heart rate changes with exercise.

MEASURING WORKLOAD

Measuring internal workload

Unlike external workload, which measures what the horse is doing, internal workload reflects how well the horse's body is coping with the exercise demands. It can be measured in the following ways:

- **Heart rate monitoring** – there are a number of heart rate monitors available to measure this easily in the horse, including those by Polar and Equimetre.
- **Blood lactate levels** – along with heart rate, this can provide objective data on cardiovascular and metabolic strain. Blood lactate levels can only be measured by your vet, so are unlikely to be monitored on a regular basis in most horses.
- **Respiratory rate** – this is a a simple way to measure cardiovascular strain, and doesn't involve the need for any equipment as it can be observed. Watch the horse's flank (the slightly indented area between the ribs and the hindquarters) and observe the rise and fall of the body to indicate one full breath. Use a stopwatch and count the number of breaths in 15 seconds, then multiply by 4 to get breaths per minute (bpm). The resting respiratory rate for a horse is between 8-16 bpm, which can raise significantly during exercise but should return to normal in 10-20 minutes. An elevated respiratory rate for longer than this may indicate that the workload is too high for the horse's current fitness level.

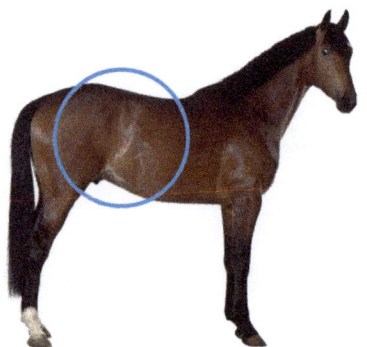

The horse's flank (circled) is the area from which you can measure their respiratory rate

- **RPE (Rate of Perceived Exertion)** – In people, this is a subjective measure of how hard someone feels that they are working during physical activity. It is typically assessed along a scale of 0-10, with 0 indicating no feeling of exertion and 10 the highest possible feeling of effort. An example of the scale used in people is as follows:

1	**Very light activity** (it doesn't even feel like you're exercising, step up from complete rest)
2-3	**Light activity** (it's easy to breathe and have a conversation, could maintain for hours)
4-6	**Moderate activity** (able to talk and hold short conversation, could maintain for long periods)
7-8	**Vigorous activity** (short of breath – you can speak, but only a sentence at a time)
9	**Very difficult activity** (difficult to maintain exercise intensity, hard to speak more than one word)
10	**Maximum effort activity** (feels impossible to continue – completely out of breath, unable to talk)

MEASURING WORKLOAD

Since horses can't self reflect in the same way, equine RPE is estimated by the rider/trainer based on observed signs. It's important to remember this is a subjective measure, so works best if the same person awards the score each time. Consider factors such as temperature and environmental stressors, which will influence sweat and behaviour.

> **Observed signs that can be used to assess RPE in the horse**
>
> **Respiratory signs:**
> - Increased respiratory rate (faster breathing)
> - Laboured or heavy breathing
> - Flared nostrils
> - Prolonged recovery time to return to normal breathing
>
> **Behavioural signs:**
> - Reluctance to move forward or respond to aids
> - Tail swishing or head tossing
> - Increased distractibility or signs of stress, such as shying
>
> **Physical signs:**
> - Excessive sweating (especially in cool weather or at low-intensity exercise)
> - Altered gait or fatigue-related changes in movement, such as loss of rhythm or shortened stride length
> - Stumbling or tripping
> - Increased heart rate or prolonged recovery
> - Change in posture
> - Stiff or uneven movement

SAMPLE TRAINING LOG

Basic Information
- Date: _____
- Horse Name: _____
- Rider/Trainer: _____
- Discipline: _____
- Weather Conditions: _____

Session Details
- Total Duration (min): _____
- Estimated Distance (if known): _____ km/miles
- Surface Type: (circle one)
  - Firm Grass / Soft Grass / Sand / Synthetic / Road / Other: _____
- Terrain: (circle all that apply)
  - Flat / Hills / Mixed

Gait & Effort Tracking
Time Spent (min)
Notes (e.g., intensity, surface, resistance)

Walk _____

Trot _____

Canter _____

Gallop _____

Workload Indicators
- Number of Jumps: _____ (if applicable)
- Number of Transitions: _____
- Sweat Level (circle one): None / Light / Moderate / Heavy
- Breathing Recovery Time (post-exercise): _____ min (time until normal breathing returns)
- Signs of Fatigue/Resistance: (circle all that apply)
  Faster breathing   Heavy Breathing   Flared nostrils   Prolonged recovery time   Reluctance to continue
  Tail swishing   Head tossing   Shying   Napping   Pigrooting   Bucking   Rearing   Excessive sweating
  Loss of rhythm   Shortened stride   Stumbling   Tripping   Loss of balance   Loss of frame
  Stiff/uneven movement   Falling in or out

Rider's Perceived Effort (RPE scale 1-10)
- 1 = Very Light Activity
- 2-3 = Light Activity
- 4-5 = Moderate Activity
- 6-7 = Vigorous Activity
- 8-9 = Very Hard Activity
- 10 = Max Effort
- RPE Score: _____

Additional Notes: _____
_____
_____

QUANTIFYING TRAINING LOAD

When applying a score to quantify training load, it helps to consider both the magnitude (how hard the work is) and the frequency of loads (how often they occur).

This diagram shows how the size (magnitude) and frequency of training loads can affect the horse. The vertical axis represents how hard or intense the work is, while the horizontal axis shows how often it's done, either in number of repetitions or the length of the session.

In the middle of the graph is the "safe zone," where training loads are appropriate for the horse's current fitness. Loads below this zone will be too light to maintain or build fitness. Loads above the safe zone are higher training loads that the horse is not accustomed to. They might include sessions that include work at a higher intensity than the horse is used to, or doing high-intensity work more frequently or for a longer period of time. This red zone indicates loads that may exceed the strength of the horse's bone or soft tissues and thus increase the risk of injury.

For example, a high-intensity activity like a 1.3m showjumping round should be done less often or for a shorter duration to stay within safe limits. On the other hand, low-intensity work like hand-walking can be done more often and for longer periods without overloading the horse. Both can fall within the safe zone when managed well. In contrast, box rest doesn't provide enough load to maintain tissue strength and sits below the safe zone.

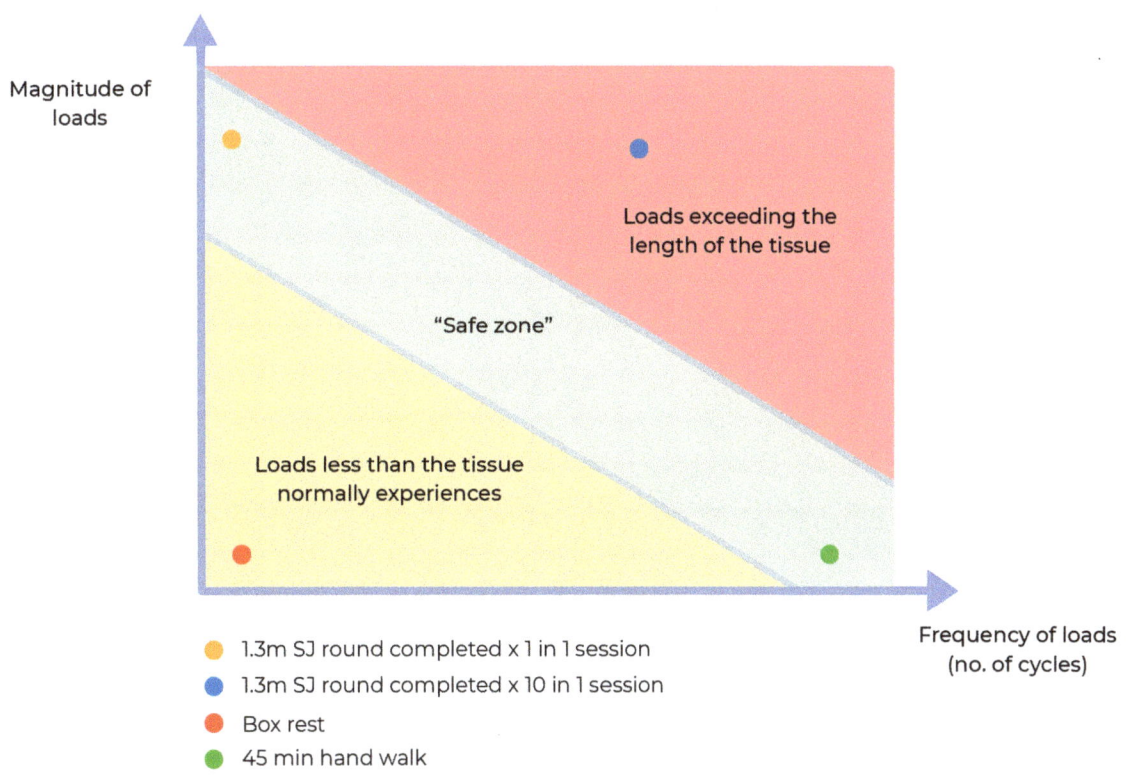

QUANTIFYING TRAINING LOAD

In this example, a 1.3m showjumping round falls within the safe zone when performed once, assuming the horse is fit and appropriately conditioned for that height. However, repeating the same course 10 times in one training session will likely push it into the unsafe zone, as the combination of high magnitude and high frequency increases the load on the tissues.

On the other hand, if walking is the chosen exercise, it needs to be done more frequently or for longer durations to stimulate tissue adaptation. Thinking about exercise in this way shows there's no universally right or wrong activity. What matters is prescribing it appropriately.

ACUTE:CHRONIC WORKLOAD RATIO

The Acute:Chronic Workload Ratio (ACWR) is a concept from human sports science that helps track how prepared an athlete is for performance and how their training might relate to injury risk. While it has its critics, most experts agree that it can be a helpful tool for monitoring workload over time. For horse owners and trainers, it offers a simple way to get a clearer picture of how much work an individual horse is doing, and whether that workload is increasing or decreasing in a potentially risky way.

What is it?

The ACWR compares how much work your horse has done in the past week (known as the acute workload) with the average weekly workload over the previous four weeks (the chronic workload).

$$\frac{\text{Acute Workload (past week)}}{\text{Chronic Workload (average of last 4 weeks)}}$$

- If the result is 1.0, your horse is doing the same amount of work as usual.
- If it's over 1.0, workload has increased.
- If it's under 1.0, workload has decreased.

Research suggests an optimal ACWR falls between 0.8 and 1.3. Too high or too low can increase injury risk.

Putting into practice

Let's assume we are monitoring a horse in training for a short endurance ride. In the past seven days, they did a total of 13km in training rides spread over four days (acute workload) and in the previous four weeks the distance ridden was an average of 10.25km each week (chronic workload). This was calculated as follows:
Week 1 (9km) + Week 2 (10km) + Week 3 (11km) + Week 4 (11km)
4 week average = 10.25 km

To calculate the ACWR, we divide the acute workload (13 km) by the chronic workload (10.25 km), which results in an ACWR of 1.27. This indicates that the horse performed 127% of the workload in the past week compared to the average workload over the previous four weeks, reflecting a 27% increase in workload.

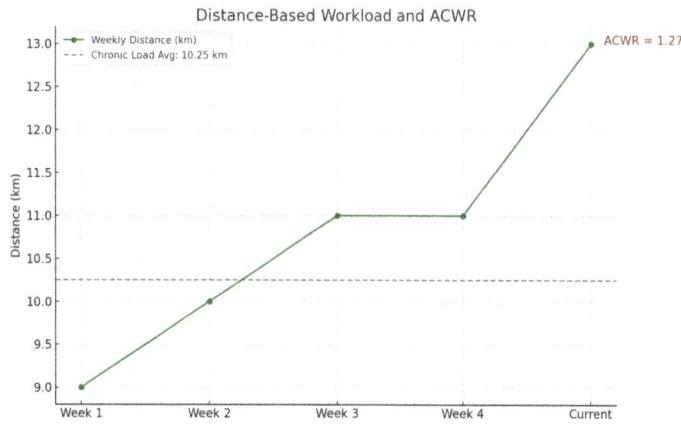

ACUTE:CHRONIC WORKLOAD RATIO

As you can see in this example, we're only measuring external training load by distance. This approach can be limiting, as it doesn't fully represent the true intensity of the training. A session duration or distance may include periods spent in different gaits, but this isn't accounted for in the current method. For example, let's say that over the past four weeks, the horse has covered an average of 10.25 km per week, but all of those sessions were primarily at the walk and trot. In contrast, if in the last week, the horse did 13 km in training, but those sessions were predominantly at trot and canter, the actual training load has increased significantly. Simply using distance to measure workload would show an increase of only 27%, but this doesn't reflect the true intensity of the sessions, which would be much greater than that.

A common method utilised in human sports science is to multiply the session rating of perceived exertion (RPE) by session duration or distance. Let's say that in calculating the same acute workload as above, we added a RPE score to each day. On day one, horse and rider completed a 3km ride and the rider awarded a RPE of 5 (moderate effort). The horse's workload for the day would be 15 arbitrary units (AU) (3 x 5 = 15). This process is then replicated for each training day and event undertaken during the week you are calculating. By including the RPE as a measure of internal workload, combined with the distance measure, we can obtain a more accurate measure of workload.

You could choose any measure to include here, as long as you use the same method to calculate the workload score each time. Heart rate or session duration could be substituted for RPE and distance in the example above. Some people choose to award a scoring system to a session. For example, in a 30 minute flatwork session the horse does:
- 15 minutes in walk
- 10 minutes in trot
- 5 minutes in canter

An "effort" score can be applied to this, in which the time in each pace is multiplied by the "effort" of each pace. This is an arbitrary number you can choose, as long as you use it consistently each time you measure. For example, the effort score for each pace could be as follows:
- walk = 1 (15 minutes x 1 = 15 AU)
- trot = 2 (10 minutes x 2 = 20 AU)
- canter = 4 (5 minutes x 4 = 20 AU)
- Total score for the session = 55 AU

You then apply this method of scoring to each training session, adding the total of each session together to give you your weekly workload score.

ACUTE:CHRONIC WORKLOAD RATIO

Let's take the same horse training for a short endurance ride and do a more detailed score. This time, instead of just looking at distance, we're going to combine it with an effort rating that awards a score for time spent in each gait. We do this by multiplying the effort score by the distance covered in each session.

To keep it simple, each gait is scored as follows:
- Walk = 1 point per minute
- Trot = 2 points per minute
- Canter = 4 points per minute

When we combine the distance covered with the effort score, we get the following data:
- Day 1: 20 min walk, 2 min trot = 24 points × 3.5 km = 84AU
- Day 2: 15 min walk, 15 min trot, 1 min canter = 49 points × 4.0 km = 196AU
- Day 3: 25 min walk = 25 points × 2.0 km = 50AU
- Day 4: 20 min walk, 5 min trot = 30 points × 3.5 km = 105AU

Total workload score for the week (acute workload) = 435AU

The scores for the previous four weeks, in which the horse spent more time in trot and canter, were as follows:
- Week 1: 650AU, Week 2: 700AU, Week 3: 720AU, Week 4: 799AU

4-week average (chronic workload) = 717.25AU

To calculate the ACWR we divide acute workload by chronic workload
$$435 \div 717.25 = 0.61$$

With this method of scoring, we obtain an ACWR of 0.61. Previously, when we only used distance covered as our measure, we got a score of 1.27. That's very different! What this means is that if we had only looked at distance, we would have concluded that the horse increased its workload by 27% this week, with an ACWR of 1.76, a level that falls within the suggested optimal training range of 0.8 to 1.3. However, when we applied a more detailed scoring system that factored in both the intensity (time spent at each gait) and the distance, we found that the ACWR was much lower. This means the horse performed 61% of its typical workload, which sits below the optimal range to maintain its fitness level. While such a drop might be appropriate during a planned rest or recovery phase, if the horse continued to have such fluctuations during their regular training, it could lead to de-conditioning and increase the risk of injury. This highlights how relying on one variable alone can give a misleading impression of workload. Being specific in your scoring provides a much clearer picture of what the horse actually did and supports better informed training decisions.

ACUTE:CHRONIC WORKLOAD RATIO

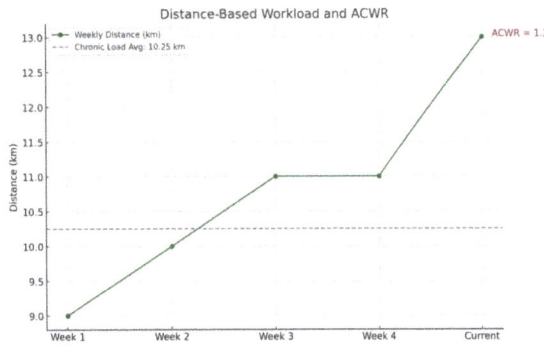
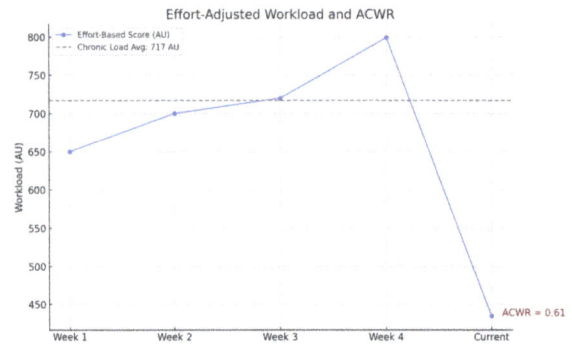

A comparison of two calculations of the same horse, on the left calculating distance only, and on the right combining distance with an effort rating to get a more accurate score of workload. This highlights the importance of not just using distance or time to measure workload, you must also include intensity.

Key Points

- Training load isn't just about distance – two sessions with the same distance can have very different intensities depending on the gait and effort involved.
- Use multiple factors to assess workload – things such as gait, time spent at each pace, and perceived effort gives a much clearer picture of the horse's training load.
- More detailed scoring gives better insights – tracking only distance or time may over-or underestimate workload, while combining effort and duration helps avoid misleading conclusions.
- Consistency matters – Whatever method you use to score sessions (e.g. effort scores, RPE, heart rate), use it consistently across all sessions to track trends accurately.

ACUTE:CHRONIC WORKLOAD RATIO

What does the research say?

There is plenty of research on using ACWR in human athlete training, but at the time of publishing, only one that has looked at it in horses. This study focused on elite eventing horses and explored how changes in training load might relate to injury risk. It included data from 58 horses over 94 competition seasons.

The researchers looked at two types of workload:
- External workload – how far and how fast the horses moved, especially at high speeds.
- Internal workload – how hard the horse was working, based on heart rate and session duration.

They tracked training and competition work, then calculated the ACWR to see if sudden changes in load were linked to injury.

They found that:
- The main risk for soft tissue injury came from sudden spikes in workload, especially in relation to how much high-speed work was done over a short period of time.
- Horses consistently training and competing at a higher level had no change in injury risk.

In other words, it's not the overall workload that's risky, it's how quickly the workload rises that can increase the risk of injury. These findings line up with what we already know from human sports science, in that gradual, consistent training is safer, while sharp increases in workload raise the risk of injury. This study supports the idea that tracking and managing training load can help design safer training plans and keep horses sounder for longer.

What happens when there is a sudden spike in training load?

A spike in training load happens when a horse suddenly performs significantly more work or at a higher intensity than it has been accustomed to. Spikes can occur during competition, training camps or clinics. This sharp increase can place extra strain on muscles, tendons, and bones, and is linked to a higher risk of injury.

Let's say we calculate scores for a horse's training sessions each week based on session duration × intensity measured as RPE. The sessions for chronic load are calculated as follows:

ACUTE:CHRONIC WORKLOAD RATIO

Chronic load (average score over past 4 weeks):

- Week 1 = 565
  - Mon: 45 (min) x 5 (RPE) = 225
  - Wed: 30 (min) x 6 (RPE) = 180
  - Fri: 40 (min) x 4 (RPE) = 160

- Week 2 = 480
  - Mon: 30 (min) x 5 (RPE) = 150
  - Wed: 40 (min) x 3 (RPE) = 120
  - Fri: 35 (min) x 6 (RPE) = 210

- Week 3 = 585
  - Mon: 45 (min) x 6 (RPE) = 270
  - Wed: 30 (min) x 5 (RPE) = 150
  - Fri: 40 (min) x 4 (RPE) = 160

- Week 4 = 625
  - Mon: 35 (min) x 7 (RPE) = 245
  - Wed: 40 (min) x 5 (RPE) = 200
  - Fri: 30 (min) x 6 (RPE) = 180

RPE Scores		
	1	Very light activity (it doesn't even feel like you're exercising, step up from complete rest)
	2-3	Light activity (it's easy to breathe and have a conversation, could maintain for hours)
	4-6	Moderate activity (able to talk and hold short conversation, could maintain for long periods)
	7-8	Vigorous activity (short of breath – you can speak, but only a sentence at a time)
	9	Very difficult activity (difficult to maintain exercise intensity, hard to speak more than one word)
	10	Maximum effort activity (feels impossible to continue – completely out of breath, unable to talk)

Chronic load = (565 + 480 + 585 + 625) / 4 = 563.75

Acute load (Week 5) – horse attends a 3 day eventing clinic

- Week 5: 1230
  - Fri: 60 (min) x 7 (RPE) = 420
  - Sat: 45 (min) x 8 (RPE) = 360
  - Sun 75 (min) x 6 (RPE) = 450

Acute:Chronic Workload Ratio = acute load/chronic load
1230/563.75 = 2.18

An ACWR of over two means the horse suddenly worked more than twice as hard in terms of load compared to what it was used to over the past month. This is a big spike in training load and has been linked to higher injury risk in human studies.

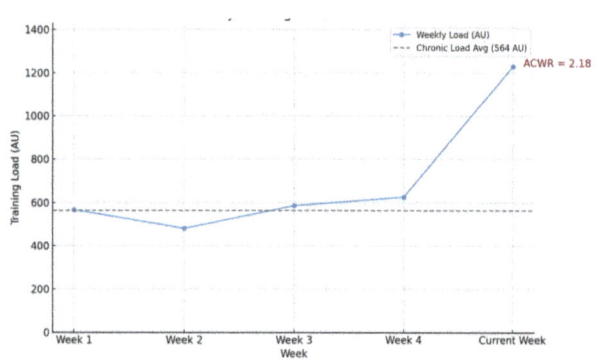

ACUTE:CHRONIC WORKLOAD RATIO

When a spike is caused by competition

As in the example above, competitions or clinics naturally push the horse harder. This may be due to longer periods of time spent training, higher speeds or greater intensity leading to a sharp increase in internal and external load.

Even if training is well-managed, a single competition week can double the usual load and push the ACWR well above 1.5–2.0. While that doesn't necessarily mean that anything bad will happen to the horse or that injury is guaranteed, it is possible that it will increase the risk of injury.

Examples of how to mitigate the risk of injury due to this include:

1. Progressive loading before competition
- Gradually increase training intensity and volume in the 2-3 weeks leading up to the event.
- This builds chronic load so the ACWR spike isn't as steep when the competition hits.

2. Include "competition-like" sessions
- Mimic elements of the event in training (e.g., gallops, jumps, terrain, higher heart rate intensity). To do this incorporate 1-2 sessions per week that mimic key aspects of the event. Aim to schedule the sessions 3–7 days before a major event, adjusting the timing based on your horse's fitness and the discipline. For example, dressage can be done closer to the event, while cross-country or high-intensity gallop sessions require a longer lead-in for adequate recovery. During these sessions match expected heart rate or RPE (e.g., RPE 7-8/10).
- Follow each session with 1-2 lower intensity days (such as flat work or a hack out) for recovery. Ensure you don't schedule competition-like sessions on consecutive days.
- This helps the horse physiologically prepare and reduces the shock load on the day/s of competition.

3. Plan a deload/recovery period after competition
- Lower the intensity and volume for at least 24-72 hours post-event.
- This allows for recovery and helps bring the ACWR back into a safer range.

4. Use ACWR proactively
- Monitor weekly, and flag when acute load becomes greater than 1.5 on a regular basis.
- Adjust sessions accordingly – for example, reduce high-speed work before or after competition weeks.

5. Watch for cumulative stress
- If competitions are frequent (back-to-back weekends), even smaller spikes can compound increases in ACWR and injury risk, especially if recovery is incomplete.

ACUTE:CHRONIC WORKLOAD RATIO

What happens to the ACWR when you include a taper week before a big competition?

Tapering is when you gradually reduce a horse's exercise before a competition to ensure they are not fatigued and are able to perform at their best. It can give the body time to recover and repair, especially when the training intensity in preparation for an event may have been high. At its simplest, it means that you ease off the workload in the days or weeks leading up to the event. This should be done taking into account the individual horse's fitness, behaviour, environment and past performance.

Managing ACWR can actually be tricky when tapering before competition. The taper week lowers the ACWR temporarily, and then the competition spikes it dramatically the following week. The challenge with interpreting this is that the ACWR doesn't account for the idea of tapering. It only sees reduced load followed by a big spike, which it flags as risky. But as tapering is deliberate, this isn't necessarily a training error, unless the spike is too big or the chronic load wasn't sufficient beforehand.

We can account for this in several ways:
1. **Build chronic load before tapering**
    - This ensures that the ACWR doesn't spike too much post-taper.
    - To do this, make sure your training load in the 1-2 months prior to competition is gradually building up (within recommended levels of ACWR 1.1-1.3)

2. **Taper, but don't completely shut down**
    - Many riders do this by shortening the duration of the sessions, while maintaining the same level of intensity. This can ensure that the horse stays switched on and prepared for competition, while allowing time for more recovery and rest.

3. **Interpret ACWR alongside context**
    - Use it as a tool, not a rule. The numbers need to be interpreted based on what you're actually doing in training.

Chapter 4

MONITORING FOR EARLY SIGNS OF INJURY

Understanding when to modify training or seek help

MONITORING GAIT

An outcome measure is an objective way to assess progress and determine if training goals are being met. They can also be invaluable in injury management to help identify potential issues early and assess recovery, allowing you to detect signs of overtraining.

Gait/movement

A significant lameness is easy to detect, prompting you to immediately call your vet. Typical signs include a reluctance to move, obvious favouring of one limb or the classic "head bob" at trot. However, a subtle lameness can be hard to detect and owners often miss some of the signs which suggest a lameness is present. It's important to regularly assess your horse's movement to help you identify any changes from their "normal".

Ways to do this include:

- Regularly watch your horse move in all gaits from the front, back, and both sides. Use different surfaces (hard and soft), straight lines and circles to fully examine your horse's movement. A subtle lameness may only be visible on a particular surface or on a circle.
- A head nod is often seen in forelimb lameness. The horse's head and neck lift up higher when the lame forelimb hits the ground, then go down when the sound limb is in contact with the ground. Be aware that a head nod can be present in a significant hindlimb lameness too. In this case, the head will nod down lower than normal when the lame hindlimb hits the ground.
- A pelvic rise is indicative of a hindlimb lameness. The pelvis and sacrum on the lame limb will rise (or 'hitch') when the lame hindlimb hits the ground, then drop lower than normal when the sound hindlimb lands. Both head nod and pelvic rise act to reduce concussion on the lame limb.
- It can be helpful to video your horse moving so you can slow it down and look more closely to see if the horse is tracking up evenly with each limb. If you notice that the horse appears to be stepping shorter with one limb compared to another, it may be indicative of an issue that needs to be investigated.
- Listen to/record footfalls of your horse walking and trotting on a hard surface – this is easier when your horse is shod but can still be noticeable in barefoot horses. Asymmetry in the timing or sound of the footfalls may indicate a subtle lameness is present.
- Toe dragging can signal several issues, including lameness, especially if it occurs in only one limb. It may also indicate a lack of hindlimb engagement, weakness, or a proprioceptive issue (awareness of foot placement). While it can be difficult to observe while riding, a simple way to check is by looking for drag marks in the sand after a training session. If this happens frequently and with noticeable marks, it's worth investigating further to determine the underlying cause.

MONITORING GAIT

- Use a tracking sensor, such as Equimetre, Equestric, or Equisense. While these devices can't directly diagnose lameness, they measure key gait parameters, including stride length, step count, and stride frequency, using this data to assess rhythm, cadence and symmetry between diagonal limb pairs.

Any significant deviation from your horse's usual movement patterns could indicate a potential issue that warrants further investigation with your vet.

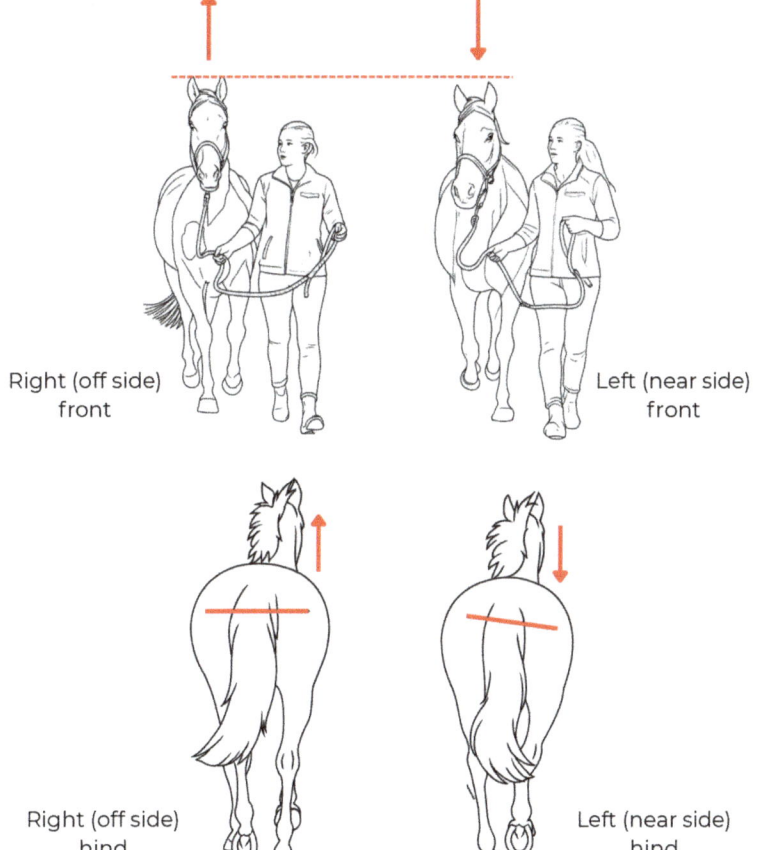

Head and neck lift up when lame limb is on the ground (right front) and lower down when the sound limb lands (left front).

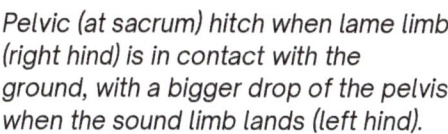

Pelvic (at sacrum) hitch when lame limb (right hind) is in contact with the ground, with a bigger drop of the pelvis when the sound limb lands (left hind).

MONITORING PAIN

Pain

While pain response and behaviours are crucial to consider for horse welfare, objectively measuring pain is extremely difficult. In recent years, researchers have taken some steps to help us better detect pain in horses through the development of several pain assessment scales. These include:

- Horse Grimace Scale (Costa et al. 2014)
- Equine Pain Face (Gleerup et al. 2015)
- Ridden Horse Pain Ethogram (RHpE) (Dyson et al. 2018 & Dyson 2022)
- Horse Chronic Pain Scale (HCPS) (Loon & Marci 2021)
- Equine Discomfort Ethogram (Torcivia & McDonnell 2021)
- Musculoskeletal Pain Scale (MPS) (Auer et al. 2024)

It is important to consider the context in which you are observing the behaviours or facial markers to determine the relevance of it. You also need to consider that like people, different horses will likely have different pain tolerances and so each behaviour will need to be considered on a case by case basis. A number of behaviours, seen over time, is more likely to indicate pain, as opposed to observing one or two behaviours briefly.

Adverse behaviours should prompt investigation for pain, as horses are rarely 'nasty' or 'naughty'. Their actions may be expressions of discomfort that we must learn to recognise.

Some common markers across all the various scales to monitor include:

- tension around the eye/eye partially closed or closed
- intense stare
- flared nostrils +/- wrinkles present
- ears held lowered, stiff, backwards or asymmetrical
- tension of the facial muscles

So you don't influence the horse and their behaviour, ideally you would observe the horse from a distance and for an extended period of time or over repeated sessions. A study investigated whether different emotional states affect the Horse Grimace Scale (HGS) to determine if they, as opposed to only pain, influence the scores. They only investigated this in a small number of horses (seven), so we do have to consider this when we interpret the results. However, they found that the HGS scores were low (> 2/12) when the horses were exposed to a new environment, grooming or anticipation of a food reward, and this did not change when compared to the control group.

MONITORING PAIN

They did find that scores were a bit higher in horses who were exposed to a situation that would induce fear – in these horses the scores of stiffly backward ears and prominent strained chewing muscles tended to be the highest. Based on these findings we can predict that in some horses, the HGS is specific in assessing pain, and the horse's emotional state is unlikely to affect the score.

Assessing pain in the ridden horse

The Ridden Horse Pain Ethogram (RHpE) developed by Sue Dyson and her research team comprises 24 behaviours. The researchers found that observation of greater than or equal to eight out of the 24 behaviours is likely to reflect the presence of musculoskeletal pain, although it's important to note that some lame horses will display less.

Horses should be assessed for approximately 10 minutes in walk, trot (including 10m circles in rising trot), canter and transitions on both the left and right reins. Collected movements can also be assessed in horses trained to do them. The RHpE has been validated in horses performing flatwork/dressage and which have been trained to work with their head in a vertical position. It has not, as yet, been studied in jumping, racing, western performance or endurance horses.

It's also important to recognise that saddle fit and the rider themselves can influence the RHpE score.

Using these scales can be challenging, and it can be difficult to be totally objective when it's your own horse. We recommend working with an experienced professional such as your vet, physiotherapist or trainer to help you in using these scales to assess your horse.

The still shots above were taken from a ridden session in which the horse displayed a number of facial and body markers. These included asymmetrical ear position, regularly changing head position, facial muscular tension, mouth open, closed eye and intense stare. This horse was soon after diagnosed with spinal pathology.

MONITORING PAIN

TABLE 1: The Ridden Horse Pain Ethogram, adapted from Dyson et al. 2018a

1. Repeated changes of head position (up/down), not in rhythm with the trot
2. Head tilted or tilting repeatedly
3. Head in front of vertical (>30°) for ≥ 10 s
4. Head behind vertical (>10°) for ≥ 10 s
5. Head position changes regularly, tossed or twisted from side to side, corrected constantly
6. Ears rotated back behind vertical or flat (both or one only) ≥5 s; repeatedly lay flat
7. Eye lids closed or half closed for 2–5 s; frequent blinking
8. Sclera exposed repeatedly
9. Intense stare (glazed expression, 'zoned out') for ≥ 5 s
10. Mouth opening ± shutting repeatedly with separation of teeth, for ≥ 10 s
11. Tongue exposed, protruding or hanging out, and/or moving in and out repeatedly
12. Bit pulled through the mouth on one side (left or right), repeatedly
13. Tail clamped tightly to middle or held to one side
14. Tail swishing large movements: repeatedly up and down/ side to side/ circular; repeatedly during transitions
15. A rushed gait (frequency of trot steps > 40/15 s); irregular rhythm in trot or canter; repeated changes of speed in trot or canter
16. Gait too slow (frequency of trot steps < 35/15 s); passage-like trot
17. Hindlimbs do not follow tracks of forelimbs but repeatedly deviated to left or right; on 3 tracks in trot or canter
18. Canter repeated leg changes in front and/or behind; repeated strike off on wrong leg; disunited
19. Spontaneous changes of gait (e.g. breaks from canter to trot, or trot to canter)
20. Stumbles or trips more than once; repeated bilateral hindlimb toe drag
21. Sudden change of direction, against rider's cues; spooking
22. Reluctance to move forwards (has to be kicked ± verbal encouragement), stops spontaneously
23. Rearing (both forelimbs off the ground)
24. Bucking or kicking backwards (one or both hindlimbs)

This table is adapted from research conducted by Dyson et al 2018. It lists the 24 behaviours from the RHpE. If a horse displays eight or more behaviours in a 10-minute period, there is an increased likelihood that the horse is in pain.

RECOGNISING PAIN

Case Study

Mr J

- 12 year old Thoroughbred gelding.
- Recently displaying some explosive behaviours on the ground and under saddle.
- Owners investigating source of pain to rule out physical discomfort.
- Owned for 3 years, ex-racehorse. Used as an all-rounder for dressage, jumping and trails. Has regular lessons with a dressage coach.

Mr J had always been a safe and quiet horse, but had recently started to show some behaviours that were both surprising and concerning to his owner.

These behaviours included:
- Rushing off and kicking out when trotting up for the farrier.
- Kicking the owner on one occasion during feed time.
- Regularly spooking at the same corner of the arena.

Mr J also started having trouble with trot to canter transitions on the right rein, with his owner describing it as feeling a little uncoordinated. This was something that he had never had an issue with in the past.

His owner had initially put these behaviours and issues down to the warmer weather and spring grass, but decided to seek the opinion of a physiotherapist to rule out any physical discomfort. It was observed that Mr B was quite difficult to handle on the ground. As he had done for the farrier, he would rush and kick out during trot up, with repeated passes highlighting that he was sound but plaiting with both hindlimbs (placing each leg directly or close to directly in front of each other).

On a circle, Mr J would track with his hindquarters to the right (outside) of the left lunge circle. He had a high and tense head and neck posture. When asked to transition to canter, the upward transition was rushed and explosive, with Mr J throwing his head in the air and bucking. His owner advised he usually liked to travel in a stretched long and low frame at trot.

RECOGNISING PAIN

Mr J was referred to his treating veterinarian for a full lameness work-up. He was found to have significant pain in both hocks and sacroiliac joints, worse on the right side of the body. His vet administered treatment, and a rehabilitation plan was set up by the vet and physio. Within 2 weeks of initial treatment, Mr J seemed to be back to his normal self and was not displaying any explosive behaviours.

There were many early signs that Mr J was experiencing discomfort, including:
- Change in movement patterns, including increased plaiting with the hindlimbs.
- Crookedness (hindquarters tracking out)
- Difficulty in trot to canter transition, which began as slightly uncoordinated and progressed to explosive.
- Change in posture and an increase in tension.
- Spooking.
- Difficulty in handling when usually very quiet.

Take-away message

Any change in behaviour or perceived 'poor' behaviour should be viewed as a potential expression of pain. Make sure that you first seek veterinary assessment. Once pain has been ruled in or out by your vet, there may be additional advice and assessment warranted with your physio, bodyworker, dentist, saddle fitter or nutritionist.

FUNCTIONAL MEASURES

In human sports medicine, there are many functional performance tests that help measure an athlete's level of function and ability. Examples include a single leg hop or double leg jump for distance, vertical jump height, sprint tests for speed and agility tests.

While there have been no formally published tests for the equine population, it is relatively simple to design your own functional tests. These are useful to monitor your horse's progress, help you to identify any potential issues, and provide information that is helpful to your vet or other equine professional.

Some examples may include:

- Counting the number of times a behaviour or symptom occurs during a session, such as tripping or disuniting.
- Assessing the horse's ability to back in-hand in a straight line by making a corridor and seeing if they step outside this on either side.
- Tight-turns in each direction to count the number of times the horse crosses over with the inside hindlimb.
- Ability to jump an increased height.
- Sectional times for endurance, eventing or racehorses.

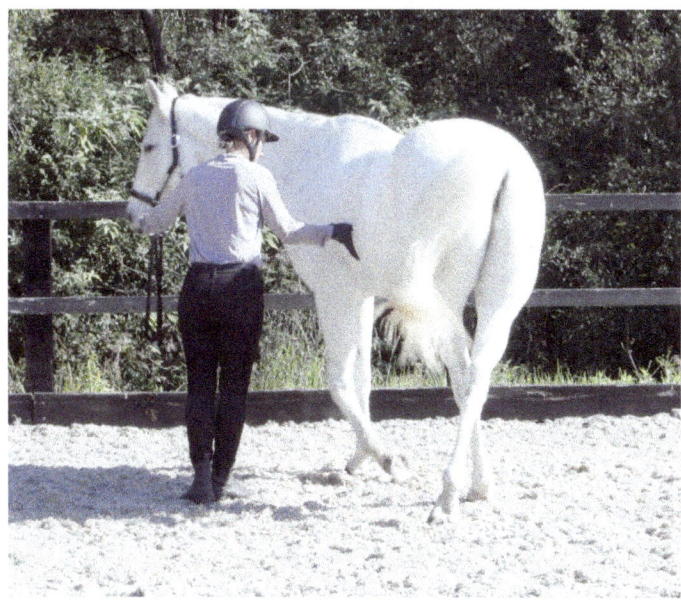

Counting the number of times a horse is able to cross the hindlimbs on a tight turn is an example of a functional measure.

Chapter 5

UNDERSTANDING THE EFFECT OF EXERCISES & TRAINING PRACTICES

Why to choose particular exercises and how to integrate them into your training

EFFECT OF EXERCISES

Research into equine exercise and sports science is steadily increasing, but compared to humans, we are still a long way behind. Researchers have started to look at the immediate and longer term effect of different exercises and equipment on the horse. This is helping us to understand the effect of each exercise and why we might choose a particular exercise for our own horse. Rather than doing the same exercises you see others doing at your yard or on social media, you can make an informed choice about the most beneficial exercise for your horse. A deeper understanding of the potential effect of different exercises, along with knowing how to best perform them, may also help to reduce the risk of injury.

In this section, we will discuss different types of ground exercises that could benefit your horse, along with the effect of circles, surfaces, speed, gradients and jumping. This can help you to know how and why to add these variables safely into your training.

STRETCHING

Stretching

Even though there's a lot of research on stretching in people, we still don't fully understand exactly how it improves flexibility. What is becoming more recognised is that one of the key changes seems to come from the body getting used to the feeling of being stretched, known as increased stretch tolerance, as opposed to the muscles actually getting longer. With regular practice, people (and we therefore assume horses) can gradually go further into a stretch without it feeling as uncomfortable. Some studies also suggest that stretching may reduce the body's natural resistance to movement over time, making it easier to reach a greater range of motion.

Static stretching and its effect on strength/power

Since the early 2000s, studies have shown that doing static stretching right before activities like sprinting or jumping can reduce strength and power in human athletes.

Research hasn't yet determined the reason why this occurs. One theory is that the nervous system reduces how strongly muscles can contract, while another is that there is a change in how the muscles and tendons work after they are placed on stretch. What researchers have concluded is that, while stretching can make muscles more flexible by reducing stiffness, that same reduction may make them less springy and powerful.

Think of a trampoline spring – firm but flexible, great at bouncing back and storing energy. Now think of a slinky – very bendy but slow moving and not good at snapping back quickly. Prolonged stretching may make muscles act a little more like the slinky, which means they lose some of their ability to generate quick, powerful movements. Now, this is quite an extreme example (a muscle and tendon will never be as floppy as a slinky!), but it provides a good visual for us to better understand the concept.

This doesn't mean stretching should be avoided. What we have learnt from human research is that timing and duration matter. Research in people shows that static stretching can reduce muscle stiffness, but the effect is short-lived, often lasting for approximately five minutes. If stretching is done immediately before exercise, especially for longer than 60 seconds, it has been shown to slightly reduce strength or power for a short period of time. This might not matter for light work, but it could affect performance in high-demand activities like jumping, galloping, or high-level dressage movements.

Shorter stretches (around 30–60 seconds) have been shown to reduce stiffness without impacting strength or power.

STRETCHING

What this research suggests is that short stretches (held for less than 60 seconds) before exercise are generally safe and may even support flexibility for most horses. However, for high-performance horses, especially right before competition or high intensity training, it's best to avoid static stretching immediately beforehand. Instead, save static stretches for after training, on rest days, or at least an hour before exercise to avoid any potential loss of strength or power.

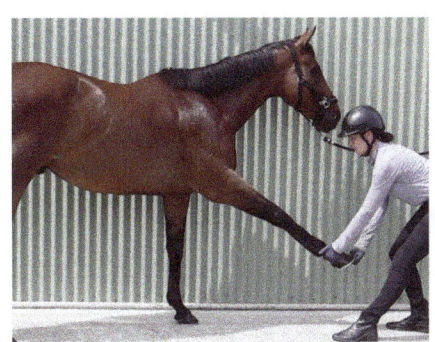
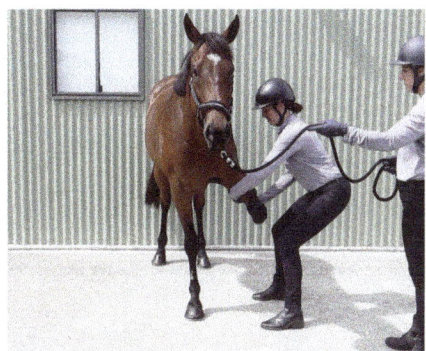
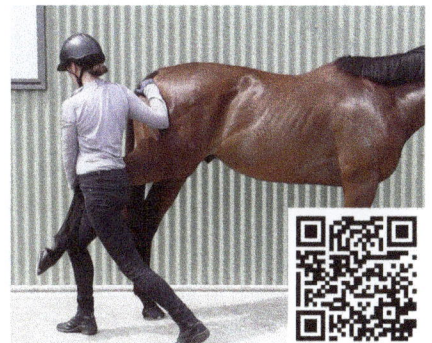

Static stretch examples include various limb stretches, such as a forelimb protraction stretch (left), forelimb abduction or "pec" stretch (centre) and hindlimb retraction stretch (right).

Dynamic stretching

Some studies in people have found that dynamic stretching can improve power and agility more than static stretching or no stretching at all. While we don't fully understand why, there are a few likely reasons. Since dynamic stretching involves active movement as opposed to simply holding a position, such as we do in static stretching, it may help warm up the muscles by raising their temperature, making them more flexible and less resistant to stretch. It's like trying to touch your toes first thing in the morning versus after a walk, it feels easier once you're warmed up. Warmer muscles may also respond faster to signals from the brain, which can improve performance.

Another theory is that dynamic stretching works like a movement rehearsal. By repeating specific movement patterns, it helps improve coordination and body awareness, Finally, dynamic stretching may also "wake-up" muscle sensors called spindles, which trigger quick reflexes and make the muscles more responsive, helping the body perform better once exercise begins.

STRETCHING

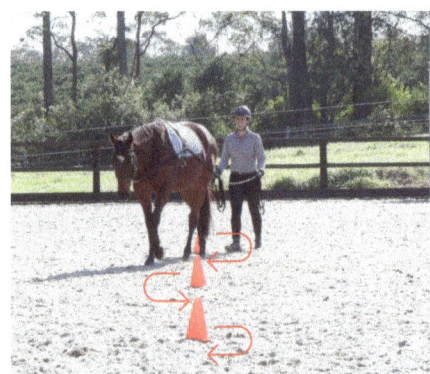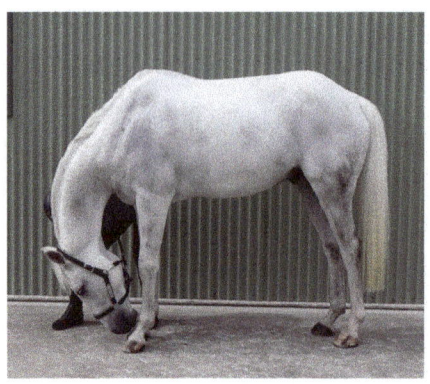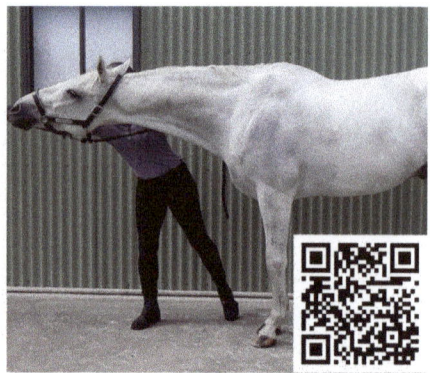

Dynamic mobility exercises can include weaving through cones or over poles (left) and moving through full range of movement in a dynamic mobilisation exercise (centre and right).

Key Points

- Static stretching is most useful after exercise or on rest days. It can help to support long-term flexibility, which may help reduce stiffness and improve movement patterns.
- Performing long static holds of stretches immediately before high-intensity work may reduce strength and power for a short time. They're best avoided immediately before competition or demanding training sessions.
- Not every horse needs to be routinely stretched! If your horse is hypermobile, stretching can actually cause more issues for your horse, including increasing the risk of injury. Focus instead on strengthening for the hypermobile horse.
- Dynamic stretching is designed to prepare the body for exercise, and as such can help improve performance, making them a great addition to your warm-up.

DYNAMIC MOBILISATION EXERCISES

Dynamic mobilisation exercises (DMEs)

Dynamic mobilisation exercises (DMEs), often called baited or carrot stretches, are used by many owners, but with little understanding of what effect they have on the horse. DMEs are often used as a stretching exercise, however, there are additional benefits. These exercises can play an important role in building muscle, improving posture, and improving symmetry.

Research has shown that doing five reps of DMEs, five days a week for anywhere between six to 12 weeks, can increase the size and symmetry of the multifidus muscle, one of the key stabilising muscles of the spine. These changes have been seen in horses out of work, as well as in racehorses.

It's not just the back that can benefit. Certain DMEs, such as having your horse bend around to take their nose towards their hip or hind fetlock, also switches on abdominal muscles. These lateral bending exercises mostly activate the muscles on the same side your horse is bending towards, helping to build strength and control through each side of the body. By understanding these effects, you can use DMEs to target particular muscle groups to help improve symmetry.

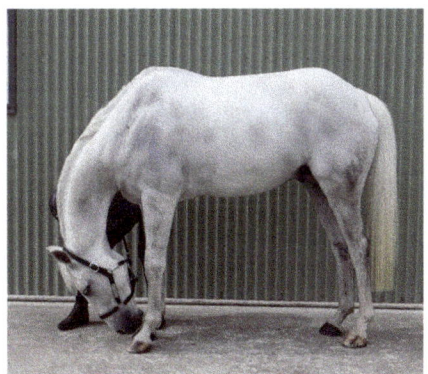
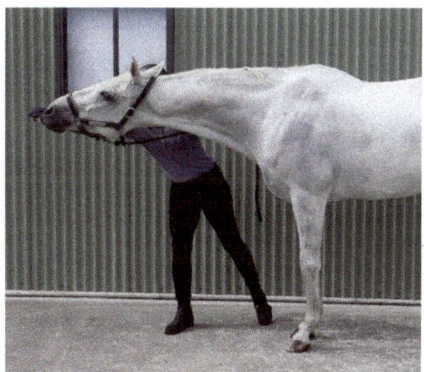

Examples of some the DMEs performed in the above mentioned studies.

How to perform DMEs

During these exercises, the horse is encouraged into each position as they follow the treat which is held at their chin region. Ensure that you are allowing the horse to move themselves and that you are not passively guiding them by pulling on the lead rope. When the position is reached, it should be held for a few seconds before returning to the start position, and then repeating the movement. For safety, it is advised that you work on ground that is level and non-slip.

DYNAMIC MOBILISATION EXERCISES

Initially, if your horse is moving their feet to get the treat, it can be helpful to have them backed into a corner so that they learn that they need to move their body, rather than their feet. Some horses become a bit too food-focused with these exercises, so use your judgement to decide if they are right for you and your horse. If performing the exercise will teach bad manners, the benefits may not outweigh the negatives. We find using a lick in a tub to be a good solution in such cases, not to mention it being a safer option to protect fingers that may get mistaken for a carrot! You can also train your horse to reach for a target, as opposed to directly for the treat.

Start each exercise with the horse standing in a balanced position. While a slight difference in foot position is ok, make sure that they have their weight balanced on each foot, so they won't suddenly fall off balance during the exercise. Be mindful of your own position during the exercise, and make sure that you won't be in harms way if the horse does happen to stumble or fall off-balance. You may like to place your spare hand on your horse's body so that you can feel if your horse is about to lose their balance. Closely observe the horse during the exercise and stop if you notice that they are struggling to perform the exercise or look to be very unbalanced.

When performing a DME, it should be dynamic. This means that you only hold the position for a few seconds, then return the horse to the start position before repeating the movement. To keep up the dynamic nature of the exercise, we only give the horse the treat once they've completed the desired number of reps. In our experience, having a horse taking its time to chew on the treat before being ready for the next one can really interrupt the flow of the exercise!

With the lateral bend DMEs you may find a difference in range between left and right sides. This can be indicative of pain or pathology, but can also be a normal variation in horses with no known issues. One study noted asymmetries amongst horse's range of motion between left and right sides of the body, both in the neck and lumbosacral spine (lower back). It's important not to force the horse further than they are comfortable to go. Take note of any asymmetries, but always allow the horse to dictate the amount of range they are comfortable with. Any significant asymmetries that don't improve over time or appear to worsen with performing the exercises should be discussed with your vet.

DYNAMIC MOBILISATION EXERCISES

Key Points

- DMEs work best at improving strength and posture if you perform repeated repetitions (4-6 reps), rather than just one long static hold. Think of it like a horse "sit-up"!
- DMEs are likely to be appropriate for most horses, however it's always best to seek the advice of your vet, physiotherapist or other equine professional before doing them, especially if your horse is injured or has a diagnosis of spinal problems, back or neck pain.
- Never perform these exercises with horses with a neurological diagnosis or showing neurological symptoms unless cleared to do so by your vet. If in doubt, always seek advice!
- If your horse appears to find these exercises difficult or struggles to maintain their balance, cease performing them immediately and seek veterinary advice.

POLES

Poles

Pole work is a popular choice among riders looking to add variety to training sessions, while improving their horse's strength and movement. A number of studies have examined how poles affect movement and muscle activity.

Trotting over poles, whether placed on the ground or raised to 11 cm or 20 cm, has been shown to increase how high the horse lifts its hooves. In other words, horses tend to lift their legs higher when trotting over poles than they do trotting over flat ground. The most notable changes occur at the hip, with a significant increase in hip flexion and heightened activity in the muscles responsible for this movement during the swing phase of the stride. Interestingly, the height of the withers and croup remains relatively unchanged, indicating that the increase in hoof height is driven by flexion of the limb joints, rather than overall elevation of the body.

In addition to limb movement, pole work also has an effect on the trunk. Both walking and trotting over ground poles have been found to activate the abdominal and spinal muscles, making it a useful exercise for building strength and supporting better posture.

Pole work also modifies the rhythm and pattern of movement. It slows the horse's gait, increases stride duration, and reduces stride length, all of which can be useful for encouraging more deliberate, controlled movement.

Importantly, research has shown that trotting over poles, whether low (11 cm) or high (20 cm), does not increase stress on the fetlock joints or surrounding soft tissues, making it a safe and effective tool for most horses. However, it is important to be aware that raised poles have the potential to increase limb asymmetry (seen as a head nod or altered pelvic rise), so monitoring your horse's individual response is essential. If you observe negative alterations to your horse's gait, lower the poles back to the ground and/or slow the gait back to a walk.

POLES

Poles can help to improve the following:

- Increase flexion range of motion of the joints of the limbs.
- Improve hindquarter, abdominal and spinal muscle strength.
- Spinal mobility, strength and stability.
- Proprioception, which is the awareness of where the horse is placing its feet.

How to perform pole exercises

- Start with poles flat on the ground. Raised poles induce greater challenges in range of motion and balance, so the horse must be able to successfully negotiate ground poles before progressing to raised poles.
- Initially begin with a single pole to assess how your horse manages, progressively adding more poles.
- Straight line poles at walk should be the starting point when you are first introducing poles to your horse's training.
- If using multiple poles, ensure they are initially spaced an equal distance apart.
- Start simple and assess how your horse manages the exercise before adding any progressions or challenges.

Setting the distance between poles on a straight line

The distance between poles will depend on the size and comfortable stride length of each horse. It is essential to practice the exercise to ensure that the distance is appropriate for your horse. Altering the distance can encourage the horse to collect or lengthen their stride.

As a general rule, distances for a horse will typically range:
- Walk: 0.8 to 1.0 metres
- Trot: 1.2 to 1.5 metres
- Canter: 2.7 to 3.6 metres

*Please note that ponies and galloways will require shorter distances.

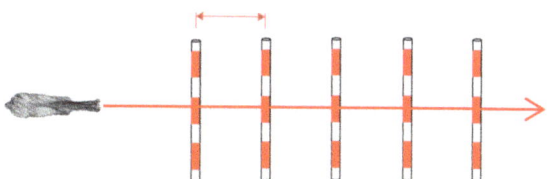

POLES

Poles on a curve

Introducing a curved line when working over poles can be a great way to challenge a horse's balance and coordination. However, it's important to understand that it's a more advanced progression and not where you should begin if your horse is new to pole work.

Benefits:

- Curves encourage lateral spinal bend, activating stabilising muscles in the trunk and pelvis that support spinal posture and pelvic control.
- Maintaining lateral bend while stepping over poles creates a higher proprioceptive challenge, helping your horse improve coordination and limb positioning.

Risks (if used too early or incorrectly):

- May encourage compensatory patterns, like falling out through the shoulder or swinging out through the hindquarters, which can reinforce poor movement habits.
- Over-challenging horses who may not yet have the control needed to manage the added complexity of a curve, increasing the risk of injury.

Start with straight lines and progress to curves only once your horse moves rhythmically, evenly, and with good posture. Begin with a wide arc and reduce the radius over time. Watch for signs of poor balance like drifting, knocking poles, tripping, or rushing.

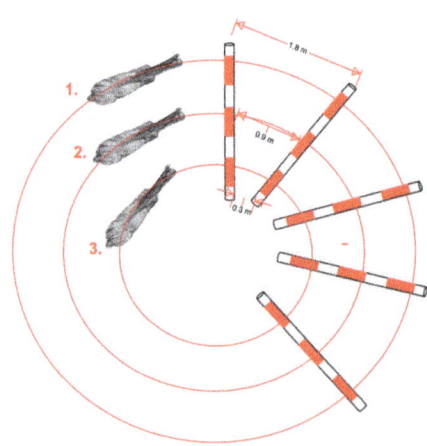

POLES

Progressing pole exercises

 *Always alter only one variable at a time*

- Increase the number of poles to improve muscular endurance.
- Increase the number of repetitions to improve muscular endurance.
- Raise the height of the poles to increase joint flexion range, strength, coordination and stability.
- Increase strength/power challenge – for example walk to trot to canter.
- Alter the spatial arrangement of the poles – for example, irregular distances (adds greater proprioceptive challenge).
- Add curves or turns (adds lateral bend through the body, challenges spinal stability and requires more complex coordination of stability at the thoracic sling and pelvis).
- Increase load through the limbs – for example, adding the weight of a rider during ridden poles to improve muscular strength.

Example of pole exercise set-up and progressions

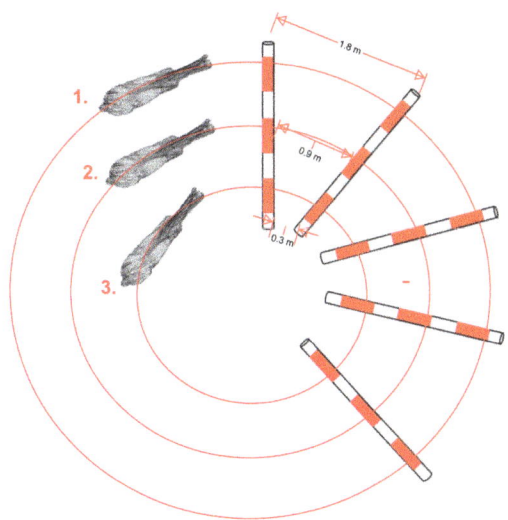

Poles on a curved line
- Inside limb requires greater flexion range during swing phase.
- Helps to increase spinal lateral bend mobility and strength.
- Progress by moving from walk through to canter, and/or by raising the inside edge of each pole on a block.

POLES

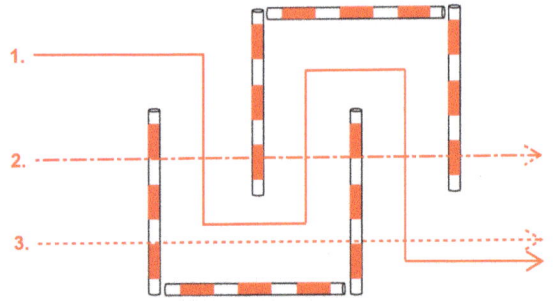

The Maze
- The turns through the poles promote increased proprioception and lateral bending.
- Perform in-hand or ridden at walk through the maze (1).
- The option to perform multiple lines (2 and 3) through the poles creates variety and reduces the need to reconfigure the poles for each different exercise.

The Snake / Slalom
- Promotes increased spinal lateral bend mobility and spinal stability through frequent change of direction
- Perform in-hand or ridden at walk.
- Helps to promote improved proprioception and coordination.
- Progress the challenge by raising alternate or both ends of each pole.

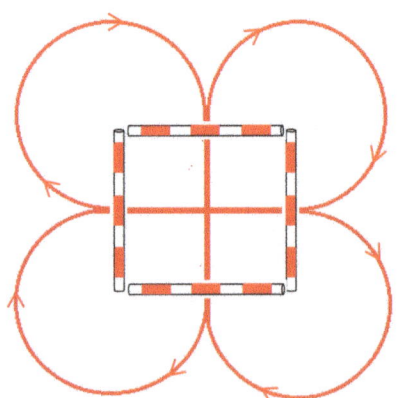

Cloverleaf
- Promotes increased lateral bend mobility.
- Consider the challenge and load of riding continuous small circles, particularly at higher speeds.
- Progress the challenge by raising alternate or both ends of each poles, and/or moving from walk through to canter.

POLES

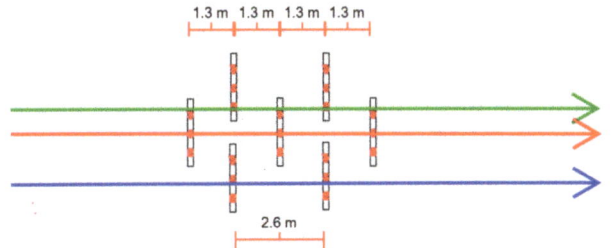

Varying Lines and Strides
- This exercise requires focus from both horse and rider to stay straight on their line, helping to improve. proprioception, straightness and control.
- This exercise is typically ridden at the trot, and could be used as a progression from straight line poles.

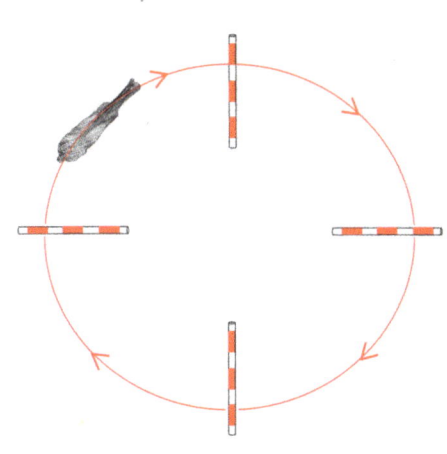

Four Poles on a Circle
- Riding through poles on a circle helps to improve rhythm and an even stride length, as well as improving lateral bend mobility, strength and balance.
- Progressions can be made be varying the circle diameter and/or moving from walk through to canter.

GRADIENTS

Gradients

Hill work is a popular and effective way to build strength, improve fitness, and add variety to a horse's training routine. In addition to making a workout more challenging, it actively influences how the horse moves, how their muscles work, and how load is distributed through their body.

Trotting uphill increases heart rate when compared to trotting on level ground, making it a good choice for developing cardiovascular fitness.

It is also a simple but powerful way to improve both strength and mobility, while also shifting weight distribution between the limbs. When working uphill, less load is placed through the forelimbs, while shifting more onto the hindlimbs. This shift encourages the muscles of the hindquarters to work harder, building muscular strength and power. It is important, however, to introduce hill work gradually and in consideration of other training practices. An example of this is introducing hill work to a dressage horse who is also training a lot of high level collected work. This could potentially overload the hindlimbs and increase the risk of injury.

Uphill work is a good example of how to improve mobility as a strengthening through range exercise. Horses trotting on an incline show greater hindlimb retraction (leg reaching further backwards), along with increased flexion of the hip, stifle and hock at hoof strike. Hindquarter muscles, particularly the gluteals, show greater engagement in order to propel the horse forwards.

How to incorporate hill work

- Begin with short uphill walks on gentle gradients.
- Progress to trotting uphill once the horse can manage comfortably in walk and has appropriate fitness.
- Keep sessions short initially (e.g., 2–4 repetitions) and increase gradually.
- Spread hill sessions across the week so they don't coincide with other hindquarter-heavy training (e.g., collected dressage, jumping).

The gluteal muscles (circled) are targeted with incline training.

GRADIENTS

Key Points

- Hill work develops aerobic fitness, hindquarter strength/stability, and joint mobility.
- Uphill work increases hindlimb load, so progress gradually to avoid overload.
- Strengthens gluteals, hamstrings, and postural muscles while promoting mobility through the hip, stifle, and hock.
- Avoid combining intense hill work with other high-load activities until the horse is well-conditioned. Remember strength training principles, and be sure to allow rest days between gradient training sessions.

SURFACE

Surface

Different surfaces can alter the horse's way of going, as well as the forces acting on their body. It's important to understand the effects of different surfaces to help you make informed training decisions, and recognise the importance of working across multiple different surfaces.

When a horse's hoof lands, it experiences a rapid braking effect, pushing down and slightly forwards into the ground. The ground then pushes back with an equal force – this is called a ground reaction force. You may remember from your high school science class Newton's third law which states that "for every action there is an equal and opposite reaction." Hard, compact surfaces (like roads or hard-packed dirt) don't deform much. That means that the hoof grips when it lands, with little to no slide (or forwards shift). This places higher concussive forces through the bones, joints and hooves. In contrast, loose or soft surfaces (such as dry sand or mud), do deform easily, allowing the hoof to slide or twist. On these surfaces, the limbs absorb impact forces more due to this slide, so these surfaces tend to be gentler on the feet and joints. However, the soft tissues, in particular the tendons, are placed under sustained load on a soft surface as the limbs stay in contact with the ground for longer. There is also a higher risk of injury on soft surfaces that allow for excessive slide or twist of the hoof.

Synthetic surfaces can strike a balance by reducing concussive forces on the limbs while still allowing for some slide, but only if well maintained and structured. Research has found that some synthetic surfaces (particularly those with a high fibre content) have too much grip, making them similar to a hard surface. On the other hand, if the top layer of a synthetic surface is too shallow or inconsistent, it loses traction, which creates less grip and more slide.

While different surface types impact the horse differently, it's important to ensure that whatever surface you ride your horse on regularly is of good quality and well-maintained. Depth, moisture content and regularity of the surface that allows for absorption of concussive forces and an appropriate amount of hoof slide, is important. A study conducted on showjumpers comparing the difference between dirt and synthetic surfaces found no discernible differences between the different arena surfaces in relation to injury risk, but they did when comparing surface maintenance.

This is not to suggest that you should only train on the one "perfect" surface type. Exposing your horse to different surfaces helps condition their body to handle a range of stresses, improve joint stability and proprioception, along with reducing the risk of overloading any one tissue repeatedly. It also helps the horse to learn how to adjust its movement to compensate for different surface types, which is especially important for horses that encounter different surfaces in competition.

SURFACE

QUICK TIPS

- Watch your horse's hoof when it lands on the surface that you train on the most. There should be a small amount of forward slide, not an abrupt stop or big slip or twist.
- Check surface depth and consistency regularly. Footing that is uneven, too deep or too shallow can increase injury risk.
- Where possible keep arena moisture consistent. Overly dry or wet surfaces can both cause issues.

Key Points

- Quality and maintenance of surface is essential to reduce the risk of injury. Regular harrowing of your arena surface is particularly important.
- Soft surfaces reduce impact stress on bone and soft tissue but increase tendon loading, particularly in the SDFT during push-off.
- Hard surfaces increase concussive forces through the limb, putting additional stress on bones, joint and hooves. However, controlled amounts of concussive force is helpful in increasing bone density and strength.
- Use gradual exposure to a variety of surfaces to help condition tendons and joints without overloading.
- Consider alternating between hard and soft surfaces to balance impact reduction and tendon conditioning.

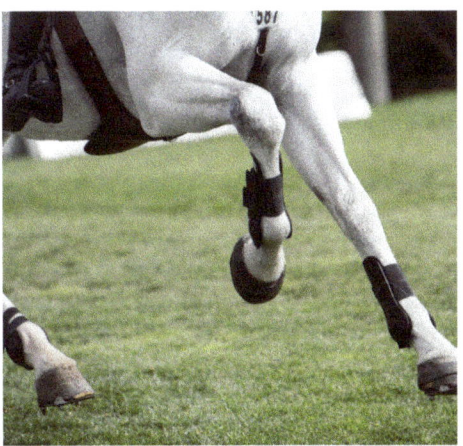

SPEED

Speed

Altering the speed that a horse is travelling will change the cardiovascular demands as well as the biomechanics – including how a horse moves, how their spine behaves, and which muscles are engaged. Speed also influences ground reaction forces, which impacts on the amount of load placed through the limbs.

What happens in each gait?

The four standard gaits of the horse are walk, trot, canter and gallop. Each gait is defined by its beat and footfall pattern, and have different biomechanical influences on the horse. Understanding these differences allows us to structure training that develops performance while minimising injury risk.

Walk

Walk is a four-beat gait, where each foot moves independently. Unlike the other gaits, there is no suspension phase. This means there is always at least one foot in contact with the ground at all times. There are relatively low ground reaction forces through the limbs at walk.

There is the greatest amount of spinal movement in the walk compared to any of the other gaits, particularly thoracolumbar rotation and lateral flexion. This is due to the fact that there is no moment of suspension, so the spine requires less stability. It is therefore a great exercise to choose when you want to improve spinal mobility.

Walk is often considered as a "rest" or "warm-up" gait, however there is much benefit in using walk as part of your training. It is excellent for developing coordination, balance, strength and range of motion without placing high loads on the body, in particular the limbs.

Trot

Trot is a two-beat gait where diagonal pairs of limbs move together. As the horse moves into trot, the hindquarter muscles (gluteals, hamstrings and abdominals) become more active. Stride duration shortens, which means the feet are on the ground for less time, and the spine itself becomes more rigid, with reduced flexion and rotation range of motion.

SPEED

Moving into a more collected trot significantly changes the biomechanics of movement compared to working trot. Speed becomes slower, and the steps are shorter and higher. The hindlimbs step further underneath the body and the hindquarters lower, carrying more weight. This is termed as greater engagement of the hindquarters. The hindlimbs act like a spring and push the horse more vertically than forward. As the weight shifts further back to the hindquarters, the hindlimbs experience a higher percentage of the total force going through the limbs (44% compared to 40% in working trot). Greater strength of the hindquarter muscles is required to maintain this position.

The thoracic sling works harder to raise the withers and forehand up, assisting to shift more weight to the hindquarters. The abdominal and back muscles also work harder to facilitate more rounding of the back and maintain the lift of the trunk and forehand. The neck position becomes higher and more rounded, requiring greater strength and flexibility.

Because of the higher forces on the hindlimbs and the more advanced body positioning, the horse requires good strength and conditioning in order to avoid overload of the tissues. Progressing too quickly to collected work, especially before the horse's body has been appropriately prepared for it, can increase the risk of neck, spinal and hindlimb injury. These changes in how the horse is required to move in collected trot need to be considered when determining how much time is spent training it.

In extended trot, speed increases and the stride lengthens as the limbs produce more push to drive the horse further forward. Research has shown that the forelimbs take on more force as speed increases, while the force through the hindlimbs remain the same. There is greater fetlock extension (or drop towards the ground) in all four limbs during lengthened trot compared to collected, working or medium trot. This places additional load on the joints and the surrounding soft tissues, in particular those of the suspensory apparatus and the flexor tendons. To avoid injury, it's important to avoid doing sustained periods of extended paces, and ensure that you don't repeat high intensity sessions that involve this kind of training on a daily basis.

The extended trot is physically demanding, requiring greater energy and cardiovascular demand. Including it in training can be an effective tool to improve aerobic fitness and endurance.

Variations in trot speed can be used strategically in training. Slower work can focus on hindquarter strength and control as well as coordination, while faster work can build fitness, strength, power, and range of motion. Be aware of how much time you spend in each speed and consider counting the number of steps or distance completed (repetitions), as well as how many times you repeat this (sets). The intensity and duration of training collected and extended trots must be increased gradually to avoid overstressing the tissues and to allow the body to adapt effectively to the training.

SPEED

In walk (left) the limbs move independently in a four-beat gait. Trot (right) is a two-beat gait in which the limbs move in diagonal pairs, with a moment of suspension in between.

Canter

The canter is a three-beat gait where the limbs hit the ground in a specific sequence. Unlike walk and trot, canter is a directional gait. This means that the sequence of footfalls is dependent on the leading leg that the horse is cantering on. The canter is an asymmetric gait, which creates different forces on each limb.

- Beat 1 – the outside hindlimb makes contact with the ground.
- Beat 2 – the diagonal pair of inside hind limb and outside forelimb hit the ground at the same time.
- Beat 3 – the inside forelimb makes contact with the ground.
- Suspension phase – no limbs in contact with the ground.

In canter, we describe leading limbs (the fore-and hindlimb on the side of the "lead") and trailing limbs (the limbs on the opposite side). If a horse is cantering on the right lead on a right circle, the right fore-and hindlimbs are the leading limbs, and the left are the trailing limbs. The limbs work together to manage propulsion, deceleration and balance. The leading right forelimb primarily slows the horse down, while the trailing left forelimb absorbs the most load and propels the horse forward. The left trailing hindlimb provides the greatest push-off force. This uneven distribution of force means that different limbs experience higher loads depending on the canter lead.

The horse's spine becomes more mobile in canter when compared to trot, with the majority of movement occurring as flexion and extension in the lumbar spine (low back).

Canter work, particularly at slower speeds, can help improve strength of major muscle groups, especially of the hindquarters and trunk. Faster canter work is useful in building both power and aerobic fitness.

SPEED

This horse is on the left canter lead. 1 represents the first limb to hit the ground, and is the trailing hindlimb. 2 represents the second beat, and involves the leading hindlimb and trailing forelimb hitting the ground simultaneously. 3 is the leading forelimb, and is the last limb to hit the ground before a moment of suspension.

Gallop

The gallop is a four-beat gait in which each limb moves and lands independently. Like trot and canter, it has a moment of suspension in which all limbs are off the ground simultaneously. Similar to canter, horses gallop on a lead. The leading forelimb is the one that lands last before the suspension period.

The hindquarter and trunk muscles generate considerable force in gallop, with the hindlimbs responsible for propulsion. The forelimbs absorb high ground reaction forces at each hoof strike, and as such are the area of the body most likely to suffer injury in horses that gallop frequently, such as racehorses. The back and limbs move through large ranges of motion, which helps to aid stride length. Stride duration is very short, meaning that each hoof is in contact with the ground for minimal time. Of all the gaits, the ground reaction forces through the limbs are highest in gallop.

A necessary part of training for racehorses, gallop training is also beneficial for eventers, endurance, polo and western horses that compete in events that require speed, such as barrel racing, reining and cutting. Gallop sessions are used to help develop anaerobic fitness and hindquarter power. Due to the intensity and high loads, gallop work should be introduced gradually. To minimise the risk of injury in both canter and gallop, it's important to vary direction and ensure the horse works in equal amounts on each lead.

This horse is in a right lead gallop. The order of footfalls is 1 left hindlimb, 2 right hindlimb, 3 left forelimb and 4 right forelimb.

SPEED

Structuring a training session

When planning a training session, you can use variations in speed as a way to achieve your training aims of improving fitness, strength, mobility, power, endurance or proprioception.

A well-structured session alternates between slower and faster work to balance load and prevent fatigue. For example, after extended trot or canter, return to a slow trot or medium walk to allow for a period of recovery, while still keeping the horse active and working.

Key Points

- Altering speed in training sessions is not only useful as a training tool, but helps to balance limb load and minimise fatigue.
- Ground reaction forces through the limbs increase with speed. Canter, gallop and extended paces place the greatest stress on the joints and soft tissues of the lower limb.
- Avoid repeating high intensity sessions that involve high speeds or extended paces on consecutive days.

CIRCLES

When a horse works on a circle, the loads through the limbs change when compared to straight-line exercise. Research shows that the inside forelimb stays in contact with the ground for longer periods of time, particularly on smaller circles such as 10 metres. This means that this limb is exposed to higher, repetitive loading which can increase the risk of injury to the joints and soft tissues of the limb.

The hindlimbs show a different pattern of loading. At trot and canter, the outside hindlimb absorbs much higher ground reaction forces compared to the inside hindlimb. The amount of this force triples when the horse moves from trot to canter. Essentially, the outside hindlimb works much harder to push and support the horse when travelling on a circle. If circle work is done repeatedly and at higher speeds, the loads on this limb can become significant.

Do you measure how much time you spend in each direction? While you may think you're spending equal time on each rein, some research has shown that riders spend more time warming-up on one rein compared to the other. There are many free GPS apps that track time spent on each rein, or you can simply record your ride and review the footage. Use this data to assess if you are training symmetrically.

Key Points

- On a circle, additional loads are placed on the inside forelimb and outside hindlimb.
- These forces increase on both smaller circles and at faster speeds.
- Avoid repetitive circle work. Track how much time you speed on each rein to ensure your training is balanced and loads on the horse are symmetrical to minimise overloading individual limbs.

JUMPING

Not surprisingly, jumping places high loads on the horse's limb, particularly the forelimbs during landing. The trailing forelimb, which is the first forelimb to land after the jump, bears the highest forces. Studies have found these loads can be twice the horse's body weight. The hindlimbs also push strongly off the ground during a jump take-off. This has been measured as three to five times more than during a normal canter.

Given the high loads placed on the limbs, particularly the trailing forelimb, it's important to monitor which lead, if any, your horse prefers when jumping. If you notice that your horse is always taking off and landing on the same lead, they are at risk of overload and injury. A study conducted in 2014 looking at the warm-up routines of showjumpers found that riders typically spent more time on the left rein. This led to a predominance in their horses for the left lead in both canter lead and jump landing.

Ensure that you approach jumps an equal amount on each canter lead. Film your sessions so that you can monitor if your horse is always landing on one particular lead. If you note that the horse consistently takes off and lands on the same lead, you can try the following:

- Practice lead changes in your flatwork, helping the horse become more comfortable and balanced switching between and travelling on both leads.
- Set fences so that the horse approaches from both leads in warm-up and training sessions. Start with smaller jumps to build confidence on the non-preferred lead.
- Strengthen the weaker side, incorporating lateral work such as shoulder in, leg yield, and travers to build strength and coordination on the non-preferred side. A stronger, more symmetrical horse is more willing to switch and travel on both leads.
- Difficulty in achieving landing on a particular lead can be due to a horse's reluctance to load one leading forelimb, indicating a potential problem. Seek veterinary assessment if you notice this.

The trailing forelimb (circled) has forces of double the horse's weight placed on it during landing.

JUMPING

Structuring jumping in your training program

Jumping should be carefully structured in order to improve strength, power and technique, while also minimising injury risk. Using the FITT principles, we recommend the following:

- **Frequency**: only perform jumping sessions a few times a week at most, following strength and power training principles. Jumping every day doesn't allow time for muscle, bone and soft tissue adaptation to occur, inhibiting strength and power gains. Overloading joints and tendons by jumping daily can also increase injury risk.
- **Intensity**: start with lower fences and less complex lines, gradually increasing height and difficulty as the horse becomes stronger, balanced and fitter.
- **Time (duration)**: continuing to follow strength and power principles, keep jumping sessions relatively short. After warming up with flatwork, poles, and small cross-rails, you might include 2-3 sets of 3-4 grid repetitions, allowing 2-3 minutes of walking rest between sets. This can be followed by 1-2 sets of 3-5 single efforts over a larger fence, again with plenty of recovery in between.
- **Type**: include a mix of exercises, such as grids, single and combination fences. Train on different surfaces, such as grass, sand or synthetic. Varying jump types and surface helps condition feet, bone and soft tissues, improves balance and proprioception and can reduce overuse injuries.

> *Key Points*
>
> - Jumping places very high loads on the limbs, particularly the trailing forelimb at landing and the hindlimbs at take-off.
> - Horses can tend to favour one lead when taking off and landing, which can cause overuse injury. Monitor your horse's jumping habits and implement strategies to encourage them to become more balanced in their jumping.
> - Don't jump everyday. A few sessions a week is best to build strength and power, and minimise the risk of injury.

PLANNING AN EXERCISE PROGRAM

Case Study

Mr B

- 20 year old Welsh Pony gelding.
- History of osteoarthritic changes in both fore fetlocks and carpus (knees).
- Retired from regular competition and training 4 years ago (pony club and low-level showjumping), to live out his life as a companion for younger horses, along with being a fun horse for an 11 year old girl to join her family on the occasional trail ride.
- Mr B is currently sound and moving well. His owner wants to maintain this for as long as possible, continuing light ridden work for 2 more years.

As horses age, it's easy to assume that stiffness, muscle loss, or reduced activity are inevitable signs of getting older. But, in many cases, these changes are not purely the result of age, but are influenced by a gradual reduction in movement and shifts in management.

Just like in humans, regular, appropriate exercise plays a vital role in helping older horses maintain mobility, muscle tone, joint health, balance, and overall wellbeing. The goal of exercise in later life isn't necessarily about enhancing performance, but about preserving comfort and function to support a good quality of life.

Understandably, some owners worry about pushing their horse too far, but in reality, gentle, consistent movement is often one of the best things we can do. A carefully designed maintenance program, tailored to the individual horse, can make a meaningful difference in how well they age. Once you understand both the effects of different exercises, along with prescription principles, putting together an appropriate training program becomes quite simple.

PLANNING AN EXERCISE PROGRAM

Mr B's situation

Mr B's owners were keen to establish a regular exercise routine for him after his retirement from regular training and competition. Since then, he had been spending most of his time turned out in the paddock. They began to notice signs of increasing stiffness and muscle loss. These changes noticeably improved after the commencement of some light, regular trail rides.

Wanting to support his mobility and condition as he aged, they decided to get some assistance in developing a maintenance exercise program. They hoped that this would benefit both his physical health, while also providing a meaningful way for him to stay connected with his young rider and continue their partnership into his later years.

Mr B had recently had a general health check with the vet, and other than some mild stiffness in his forelimb joints, he was found to be in good physical condition. His joint conditions were managed with Pentosan, along with regular trimming to maintain optimal hoof angles and limb biomechanics. His dietary needs were discussed with his vet and nutritionist to support him at this stage of life.

Which exercises were performed and why

In Mr B's case, we can keep his program pretty simple, and there is any number of different exercises we could choose that would be both safe and effective. In Mr B's case, the main priority to work on is making sure he is fit for daily paddock life activities and occasional trail rides. The areas we decided to focus on were:

1. Maintaining limb mobility to reduce signs of stiffness

We wanted to ensure these exercises weren't too challenging for the owner to perform, looking at different ways we could encourage range of motion in limbs, particularly the forelimbs. We chose:

- Walking in hand over poles – this exercise has been shown in studies to increase range of motion in the limbs. It's also a simple exercise for the handler to perform, and one that is likely a bit of fun for a younger horse owner.
- Fetlock mobilisation – every time Mr B's owner picked out his feet, she performed some gentle mobilisation exercises, moving the joint through the available range in a smooth, controlled fashion to help maintain the movement Mr B had.

PALNNING AN EXERCISE PROGRAM

- Shoulder circles – this exercise encourages mobility in all directions in the shoulder joint, along with knee flexion. While Mr B didn't have any issues with his shoulders, when horses have pathology in other joints of the limb, they can offload and compensate in other areas. This exercise also has the added benefit of being a stability/balance exercise for the opposite standing limb, which we reasoned is useful for him to work on as he ages.

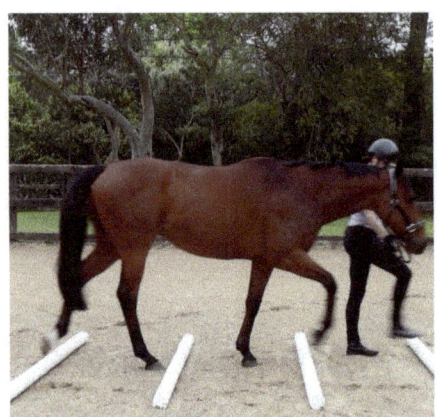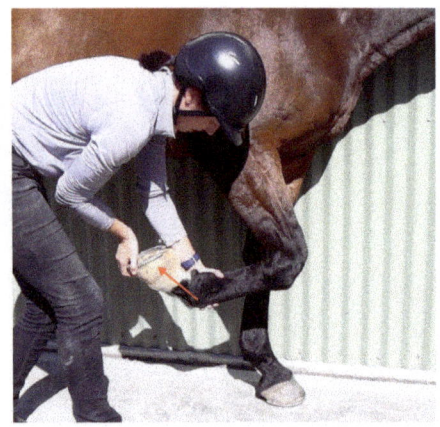

The forelimb mobility exercises (from left to right): walking over poles, fetlock mobilisation, shoulder circles.

2. Maintaining/improving spinal posture and mobility

As many horses age we start to see a change in their spinal posture. Traditionally we see this as an extended (dipped) back and sagging abdomen. But this isn't just a naturally occurring sign of ageing in all horses, often it's a "use it or lose it" scenario. That sagging posture isn't just because your horse is older, but due to a loss of abdominal / trunk strength and spinal mobility, typically when no form of regular exercise is maintained after retirement. Some exercises we included to help combat this included:

- DMEs – in all directions, but particularly those into flexion and combining lateral bend with flexion. These exercises have a double benefit of helping to keep the spine supple into flexion (to help counter the effects of the extended spinal posture), along with promoting abdominal and spinal muscle activity.
- Wither rocks – this exercise helps to activate the muscles around the shoulder and thoracic sling. It's a simple exercise to perform, so was a good choice for a young owner/older horse partnership.

PLANNING AN EXERCISE PROGRAM

- Back in hand – this exercise is a really simple way to get a number of benefits at once. It increases flexion of the lower part of the spine, and encourages transference of weight from the forelimb to the hindlimbs. Performing in a repetition, such as 5 strides back then immediately 5 strides forward, makes it a bit like a "squat" for horses!

- Poles – our pole exercise already explained above has a double benefit, as poles are also shown to help improve abdominal muscle activation.

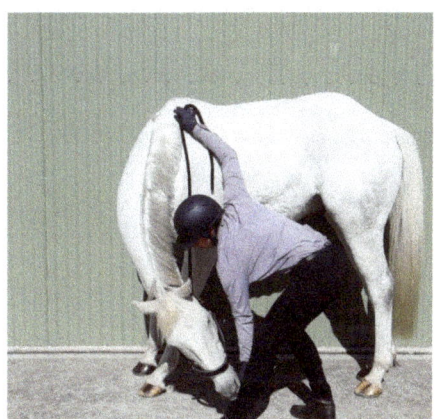 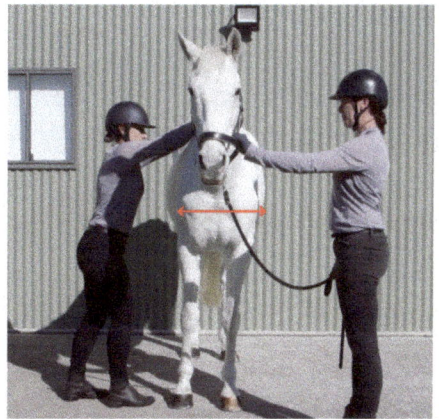 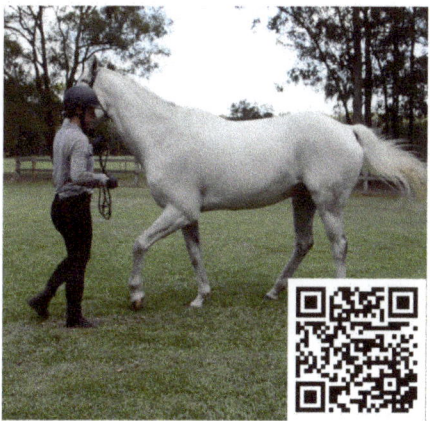

A low flexion combined with lateral bend DME (left) can help promote spinal flexion and neck lateral bend together, along with targeting abdominal and spinal muscles. Wither rocks (centre) involve asking the horse to shift its weight from side to side. Back in hand (right) helps promote greater spinal flexion and weight transference between the fore and hindlimbs.

PLANNING AN EXERCISE PROGRAM

Sample weekly exercise plan

Day	Plan

Monday	1. Ground Exercises (work into a grooming or before feeding session)
	   a. DMEs x 6 each direction
	   b. Back in-hand x 5 reps (5 strides forward, 5 strides back)
	   c. Wither Rocks 2 x 12
	   d. Fetlock mobilisation x 12
	   e. Shoulder circles x 8 each direction

Tuesday	Day off
Wednesday	1. Trail ride 45 mins – walk with small bursts of trot. Include some small inclines and change of surfaces to challenge strength and proprioception. 2. Poles – 5 poles, flat on ground, straight line x 5 reps
Thursday	Day off
Friday	Day off

Saturday	1. Ground Exercises (work into a grooming or before feeding session)
	   a. DMEs x 6 each direction
	   b. Back in-hand x 5 reps (5 strides forward, 5 strides back)
	   c. Wither Rocks 2 x 12
	   d. Fetlock mobilisation x 12
	   e. Shoulder circles x 8 each direction

Sunday	Walk over pole configuration (as above) before bringing in to feed x 5 reps

Chapter 6
BACK & NECK CARE

Monitoring and Managing Back & Neck Health in Your Horse

ANATOMY OF THE BACK AND NECK

A good understanding of the anatomy and function of your horse's back and neck is fundamental in helping you to make good training decisions and avoid injury. Understanding how the spine moves, where key muscles are located and how they function, and what effect training has on these structures will allow you to assess your horse more objectively. This awareness helps you to notice early signs of discomfort or dysfunction and to know when to seek assistance from a qualified professional.

Anatomy of the spine

The horse's spine, like ours, is divided into different regions, with a defined number of vertebrae in each.

- Cervical spine (neck) = 7 vertebrae
- Thoracic spine (mid back) = 18 vertebrae
- Lumbar spine (low back) = 5-6 vertebrae
- Sacral spine (pelvic region) = 5 vertebrae (fused)
- Caudal spine (tail) = 15-21 vertebrae (average is 18)

The vertebrae allow for mobility of the spine, as well as protection to the spinal cord and associated nerve roots. They also provide attachment points for muscles, tendons, and ligaments, and form the bony framework that connects the limbs to the body.

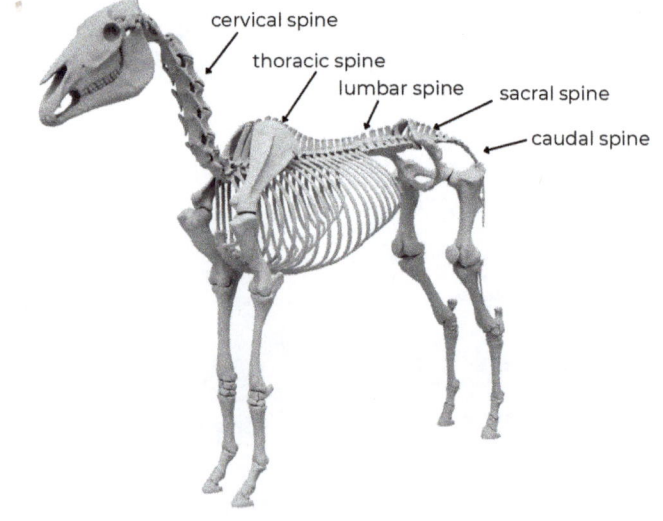

The cervical spine is quite different from the rest of the spine. It has the greatest range of motion, with vertebrae that are relatively large and surrounded by more muscle than any other part of the spine. This allows the horse to move its head and neck freely for balance and grazing. In contrast, the thoracic spine (mid-back) is the most rigid part of the spine, which is what allows us to ride them. The ribs attach to this region, forming a strong protective cage for the internal organs. The lumbar spine is more flexible than the thoracic spine. It plays a key role in transmitting the forces generated by the hindquarters, helping to propel the horse forward. The sacral spine's vertebrae are fused together, and serves as the connection between the spine and the pelvis.

ANATOMY OF THE BACK AND NECK

Muscles

The muscles of the back and neck fall into two groups, the extensor muscle chain and the flexor muscle chain. The extensor muscles run along the top of the neck and back and function to extend the spine and raise the head. The flexor muscles lie on the underside of the neck and trunk. Their role is to flex (round) the spine, along with assisting in flexing the hip. The abdominal muscles form part of this group, and they also function to hold the abdominal contents in place and assist in respiration. Deep along the horse's spine are a group of small muscles called the multifidus. These muscles act as stabilisers for the spine, helping to control and support each vertebra during movement.

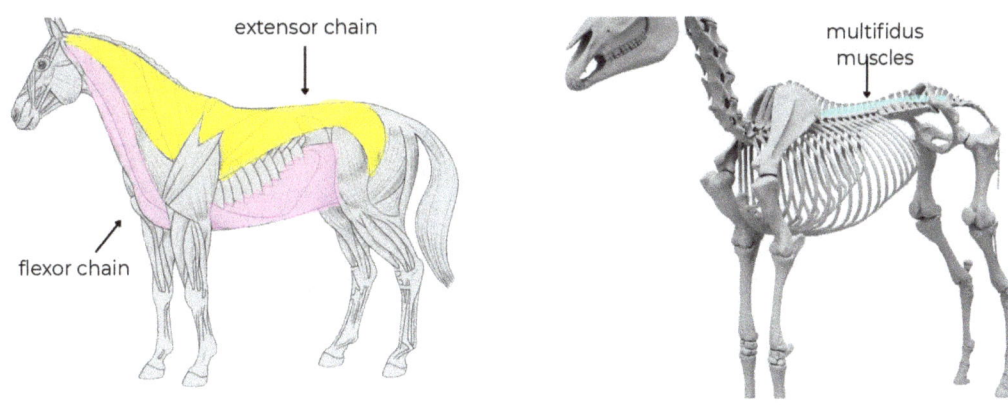

Ligaments

Ligaments connect bone to bone and play an important role in stabilising joints. Most ligaments are passive structures, meaning they don't generate movement but instead limit excessive motion to protect the joints. The spine is supported by a network of ligaments that provide stability and help maintain posture.

The main ligament along the horse's back is the supraspinous ligament, a strong, rope-like band that runs the length of the spine to connect the vertebrae from the withers to the sacrum. The nuchal ligament in the neck is quite different from most other ligaments. It is highly elastic, allowing it to stretch and recoil, which helps support the weight of the head and neck without requiring constant muscular effort. It runs from the withers to the poll and has two distinct parts:
- Funicular part: A rope-like cord running along the top of the neck.
- Lamellar part: A sheet-like structure that connects down into the cervical vertebrae.

Unlike other parts of the spine, the vertebrae in the neck sit deep beneath the surface, so the nuchal ligament provides much of the passive support. Its primary role is to support the head and neck during grazing and movement, effectively acting as an energy-saving mechanism for the horse.

ANATOMY OF THE BACK AND NECK

When a horse stretches its neck forward, the nuchal ligament puts tension on the supraspinous ligament along the back. This helps lift and support the thoracic spine, reducing the effort required by the back muscles and promotes stability of the spine during movement.

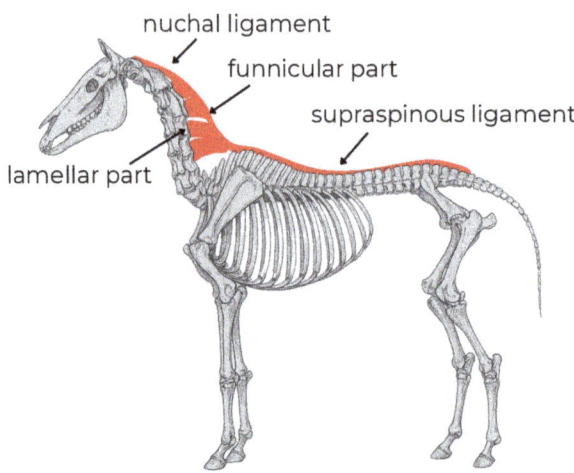

A horse's spine moves in three main directions: lateral bending, flexion/extension, and rotation.

- Lateral bending (side-to-side movement) and rotation (twisting) almost always occur together. These movements allow the horse to turn and bend during exercises like circles, lateral work, or jumping lines. Lateral bending happens most in the lower thoracolumbar region (mid-to lower back) and cervical spine.
- Flexion and extension (up-and-down movement) mainly occur in the cervical spine, lumbosacral spine and the upper thoracic spine (near the withers). These movements are important for activities like collection, take off in jumping, extending in a gallop through the back, and changing head/neck position.

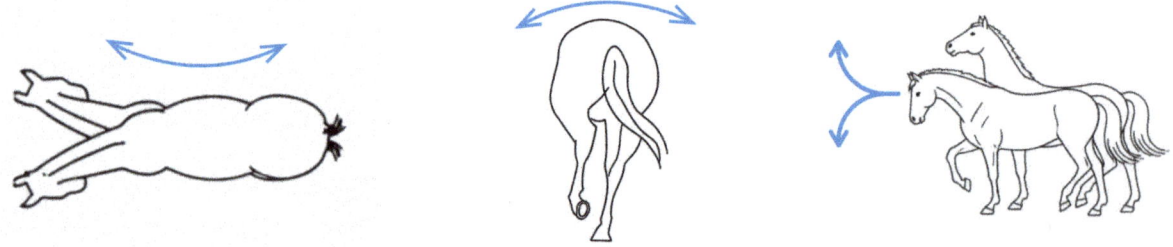

From left to right – lateral bending, rotation and flexion/extension.

BACK HEALTH

As we discussed at the beginning of the book, the saying "no hoof, no horse" is certainly true. Equally, a healthy back is just as important, especially for horses that are ridden. A horse with a healthy spine is one that is able to move freely, carry a rider comfortably and perform at their best.

Back health doesn't come down to one single factor. There are many elements that contribute to spinal health, including access to regular turnout, good nutrition, saddle fit and structured exercise. Each of these play a role in keeping your horse's back strong, supple and pain-free.

What does a healthy back look like?

A horse's back was not naturally designed to carry a rider. It is due to the relative rigidity of the horse's thoracic spine that makes this possible. While a horse's anatomy gives us the ability to sit on their back, there is much more involved for them to be able to carry a rider comfortably. A healthy back is evident in their posture, shape and muscle development.

The spine should run in a relative straight line along the horse's back. Every horse's spine will look different, and there are certain characteristics distinct to different breeds. Quarter horses, Haflingers and many breeds of ponies typically have low, less prominent withers and rounder, flatter backs. In comparison, Thoroughbreds and Arabians are more commonly known for higher or more pronounced withers and a narrower back.

In a healthy back, the bony ridges along the spine, called the spinous processes, should not be overly prominent. The muscles should be symmetrical and well-developed, appearing full and slightly rounded, as opposed to appearing hollow or tight. Running your hand along your horse's back shouldn't elicit a pain response. Signs that may indicate pain or sensitivity include dipping or dropping away from your pressure, muscle twitching or attempts to kick or bite.

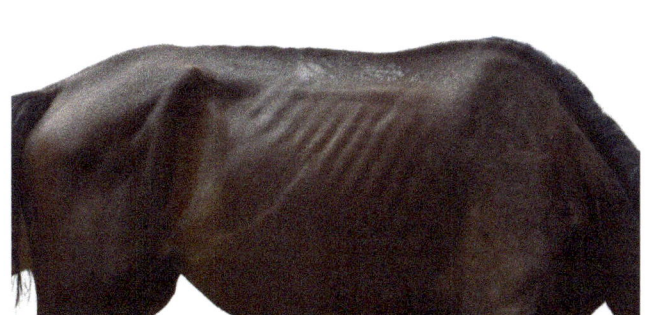 

A horse with an unhealthy back, as evident by the prominent spine and poor muscle development (left). In comparison, this back looks healthy, with good muscle covering along the topline (right).

NECK HEALTH

The horse's neck is central to their movement and balance, and issues in this area can affect their whole body. Stiffness, discomfort or pain in the neck may present as resistance to rein contact, hollowing of the back, head tossing, or difficulty bending in one or both directions. Much like the back, neck problems can arise from a variety of causes. These can include training and handling habits, dental issues, tack fit (bridle, bit or saddle), trauma, or structural changes in the cervical vertebrae. Such changes can be age-related degeneration or congenital deformities.

What does a healthy neck look like?

A horse with a healthy neck displays good mobility in all directions with even muscle development. While each horse's range of motion will differ slightly, they should be able to easily move their neck to take their nose between their fore fetlocks, towards each hip and stretching forwards and out. The neck should not be excessively fat or thin, and the muscles on both the top and underside should be well defined and symmetrical left and right.

Two neck types that are not ideal are an overly "cresty" neck or an "upside down or ewe" shaped appearance. A horse with a "cresty" neck has lumpy or hard fatty deposits along the top of the neck. While some breeds do have a more prominent neck crest, it shouldn't be hard or lumpy, which can suggest excess fat storage.

A "ewe or upside down" neck is where the muscles on the underside of the neck are overdeveloped, while those along the top are atrophied or underdeveloped. Some horses are naturally built this way, and it can therefore be difficult to change. However, in many cases this type of neck posture is due to training and postural habits. Under saddle, this type of neck is common to horses that hold their head up, are heavy in the mouth or pull along in front rather than engaging the hindquarters to push from behind.

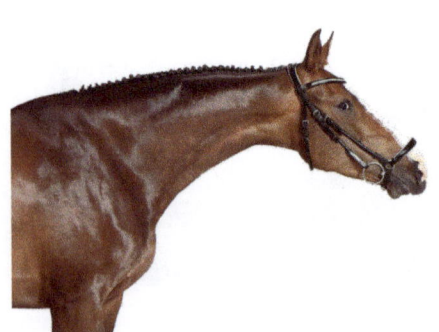  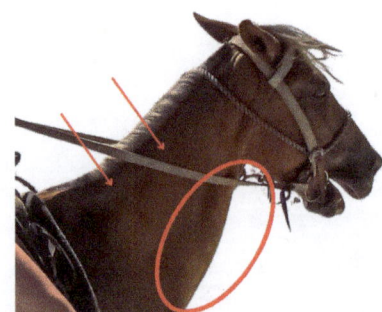

Horse with a healthy neck (left), horse with a "cresty" neck as seen by the lumpy region circled along the top of the neck (middle) and a horse with a "ewe" neck, indicated by the lack of muscle on the top of the neck (arrows) but overdeveloped on the underside (circled) (left).

BACK & NECK HEALTH

How to keep your horse's back and neck healthy

Turnout and movement: movement is key to support and promote a healthy spine. Horses are designed to move, graze and change postures throughout the day. Ensure they receive regular turnout, so they have the opportunity to behave like a horse without the restriction of a rider on their back. Anatomist Sharon May-Davis has conducted hundreds of dissections on horses across all breeds, including many on wild horses. She suggests that providing variable feeding positions in your horse's environment can have a positive effect on their body symmetry, in particular of their feet, neck, jaw and teeth. In the wild, it is suggested that horses spend approximately 80% of their time grazing (eating below knee height) and 20% browsing (eating above knee height – such as picking at trees or shrubs). These findings have led to the concept of variable feeding positions. This essentially means assessing whether or not your horse has the opportunity to eat in a way similar to the 80:20 rule, and if not, providing options in their environment to do so. Such examples include feeding hay at varying heights to allow the horse to hold their neck in differing positions or spreading hay across the paddock to encourage regular movement and stance on different gradients.

Nutrition: horses require a balance of energy, protein, vitamins and minerals in their diet to not only keep their digestive system healthy, but to help build and maintain muscle. Even a horse on the best training program won't maintain weight and condition without appropriate nutrition. Weight management is also important. Excess weight can place extra stress on the spine, while being underweight typically means the horse lacks the muscle required to provide spinal support.

Saddle fit: this is essential for any horse that is ridden. Poor saddle fit creates pressure points, muscle atrophy (wasting) and pain. We will expand on this later in the chapter.

Bridle and bit fit: there is often more focus on saddle fit, however, bridle and bit fit is equally important. In fact, research has shown that areas of increased pressure under the headpiece and noseband can impact negatively on the horse's limb range of motion. It is essential to consider bit and bridle fit for each individual horse, and we recommend working with a qualified fitter.

Hoof balance: poor hoof balance influences the way the horse stands and moves, which can place stress on the spine. Ensuring your horse has regular trims to maintain good hoof balance is essential.

BACK & NECK HEALTH

Frame and posture in training

How the horse carries their head and neck directly affects spinal posture. Research has found that horses ridden in side reins with their head held in a high position had reduced spinal mobility when compared to a lowered head and neck, altering their natural movement. Forcing a head position, or working for prolonged periods in one fixed posture, can cause muscular tension and joint restriction.

Studies have also been conducted to examine the response of horses ridden in Rollkur versus regular poll flexion (nose slightly in front of the vertical). They looked at behaviour, heart rate and a Y-maze choice test. During the test, riding through one arm of the maze was always followed by a short round ridden in Rollkur, while the other arm was followed by riding in a regular poll flexion frame.

The horses in the study showed more signs of discomfort, such as tail swishing, head tossing and attempted bucking, and slower movement when ridden in Rollkur. When given the choice to go down either arm of the maze (once the horses became conditioned to which direction meant time in Rollkur or a regular frame), 14/15 horses chose the arm in which they would be ridden in regular poll flexion significantly more often. Horses also tended to react more fearfully to external stimuli when ridden in Rollkur.

Rollkur is an extreme example, but consider that any posture in which your horse is asked to sustain their head and neck in a posture that places their nose behind the vertical can have potential implications on their movement and comfort. Variety in training and posture (i.e., allowing your horse to move between different postures), along with avoidance of forcing the head and neck into a posture through the use of either force or external aids are essential to support a healthy neck and back. We will discuss the implications of the rider's influence on the horse's back in more detail in Chapter 7.

Dressage horses ridden in different frames. A more neutral and desirable head posture, at which the nose is slightly in front of the vertical (left). Horse with a significantly more flexed neck posture, with the nose clearly back behind the vertical (right).

BACK & NECK HEALTH

Lowering of the head and neck under saddle: "long and low"

You've likely heard about a frame called "long and low". It can be a useful posture to adapt in your training, but like anything, it's important to understand the effect that it has on the horse's body to help you determine when it is appropriate to use.

What happens to the body?

When you ride the horse in a long and low frame, the following occurs:
- The horse's centre of mass moves forward, which leads to increased loading of the forelimbs and a subsequent decrease in loading of the hindlimbs.
- Greater flexion of the lower neck region, more extension of the upper neck.
- Greater tension through nuchal and supraspinous ligaments, leading to separation of dorsal spinous processes in the spine and greater flexion or lift of the back.
- Increased work of the flexor chain muscles at the base of the neck, the thoracic sling, abdominals and hip flexors.

When and why to use it?

- In order to achieve strengthening of the thoracic sling, neck, abdominal and hip flexor muscles.
- To improve suppleness of the spine.
- May provide pain relief in horses with spinal conditions such as kissing spines (always discuss first with your vet or physio if your horse has a diagnosis of this or any other spinal or neck condition).

You need to take care with how long you ask your horse to work in this frame. Like anything, spending prolonged periods in any one fixed posture isn't ideal. In a long and low frame there is increased tension on the nuchal and supraspinous ligaments, along with increased flexion of the joints of the lower neck. There is also increased load on the forelimbs. Spending too long in this frame may place excessive strain on these joints and tissues.

A long and low frame, characterised by the horse reaching their neck forward and down.

TOPLINE & POSTURE

Assessing topline and posture

A horse's topline refers to the muscles that run along the neck, back, and hindquarters. A horse with a well-developed topline shows symmetrical and toned muscles, with well-defined muscle coverage. Posture refers to how a horse habitually stands and carries themselves, including the alignment of their head, neck, back, pelvis, and limbs. Note that posture is changeable; no horse will ever have the exact same posture all the time, and they should be able to move comfortably between different postures.

Like people, there will be variations in spinal posture and conformation between horses. You'll notice differences in spinal curvature, muscle development, and body shape from one horse to another. Many of these differences are structural, meaning they are part of the horse's individual build and won't change over time.

It's important to learn what is normal for your horse so you can recognise any changes in posture or topline that may indicate pain, weakness, or developing issues. However, also keep in mind that what is normal for your horse is not always ideal. Long-standing postural habits or conformational tendencies can still contribute to pain or dysfunction, even if they have been present for years. Rather than comparing your horse to others, focus on understanding their usual posture and shape, while also considering whether these are both healthy and functional.

Some of the steps you can take to regularly assess your horse's topline and posture include:

1. Visual observation
   - Stand the horse square on a flat surface.
   - View from the side, front, and behind.
   - Look for:
     - Smooth muscle coverage along the neck (no prominent spine noticeable).
     - Even back musculature – no hollow areas behind the withers, along the neck or in the hindquarters

2. Watch movement
   - Regularly watch your horse move in walk and trot in-hand, on the lunge and under saddle.
   - Note whether your horse does the following:
     - Swings through the back, with an even shift of weight from left to right.
     - Step under their body with the hindlimbs, clearing their toes from the ground (no toe drag).
     - Carries the head in a natural, relaxed position - not inverted or braced.

TOPLINE & POSTURE

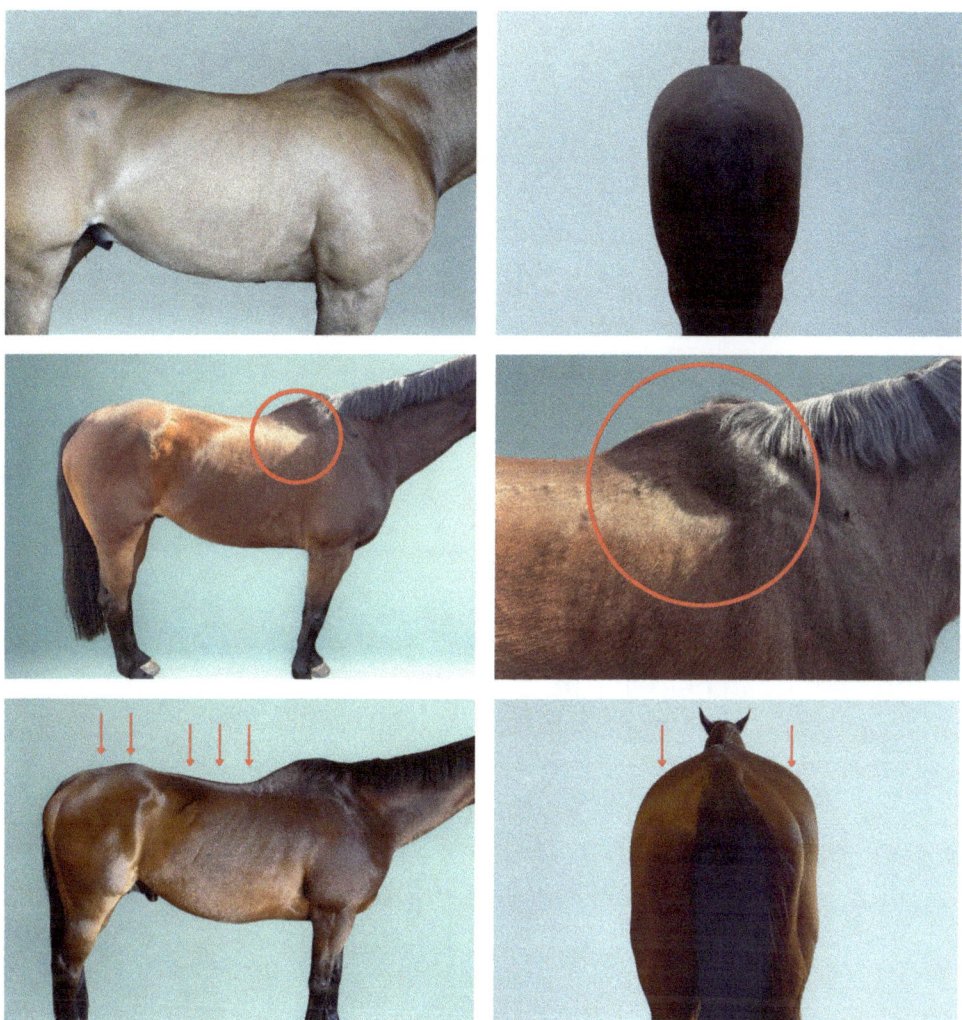

The horses on the top row are examples of well-developed topline and hindquarters. The horse in the middle row shows some loss of muscle through the topline, particularly in the region just behind the wither (circled). This horse is also showing a camped under posture with the hindlimbs. The horse on the bottom row shows a significant loss of topline and hindquarter muscle, as evident by the prominence of the spine and angular shape of the hindquarters (arrows).

3. **Look for postural habits**
   - Notice if your horse:
     - Habitually stands camped under or camped out behind. A horse that stands camped under stands with their hindlimbs further forward underneath their body, while a horse that stands camped out places their hindlimbs back out behind their body.
     - Stands with one hindlimb out to the side and/or behind, or consistently rests one hindlimb over the other.
     - Tends to hollow through the back or hold the neck high and tense.
     - It's important to note if these occur constantly, as opposed to only occasionally/ briefly.

TOPLINE & POSTURE

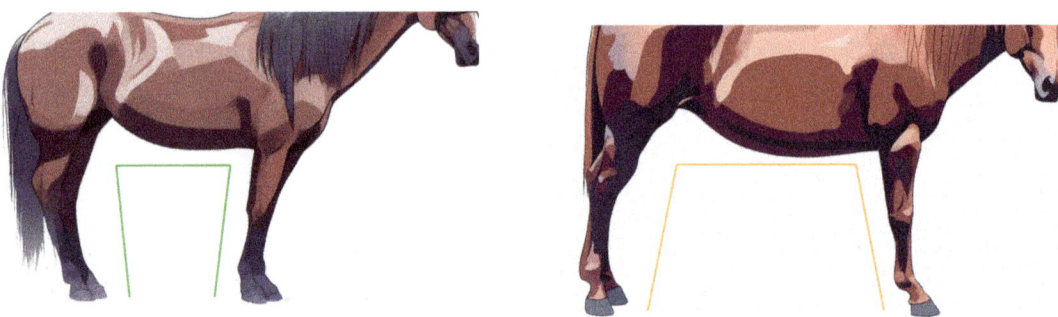

An example of a horse standing camped under (left) and camped out (right).

4. Take progress photos
- This is challenging to get accurate, and you must ensure that you try to exactly replicate the shot each time. This entails:
  - Standing the horse in the same spot every 4–6 weeks. Make sure you choose a hard, flat surface. It can be helpful if there is a fence or wall behind the side profile of the horse. This can help ensure that your measurements are consistent.
  - Ensure that the horse is standing in the same way each time, as square as possible and with head at the same height
  - Take the photo from the same angle and distance away from the horse. Changing these will significantly alter how the photo looks and will make it difficult to accurately measure any changes.

5. Use simple landmarks
- Identify key bony landmarks, such as the withers, spine, sacrum and pelvic bones (often referred to as the "hips").
- Assess whether muscles fill in the spaces between these landmarks evenly or if there are pockets of muscle loss or hollowing.

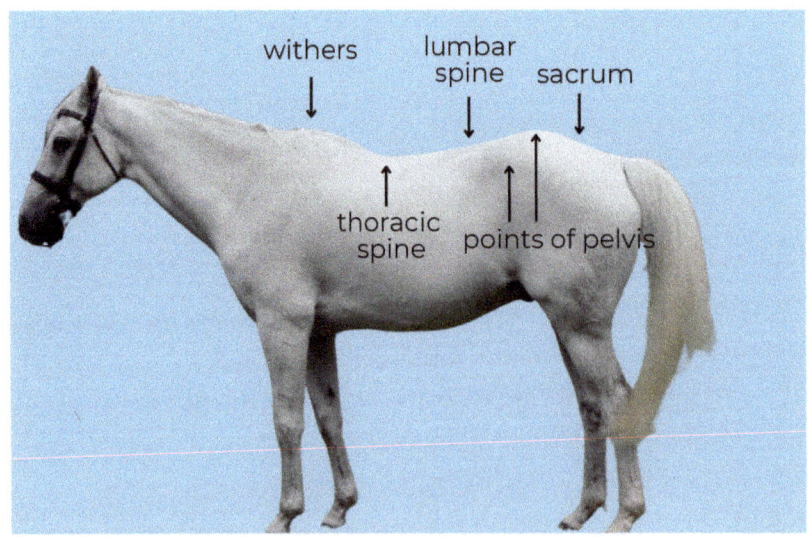

TOPLINE & POSTURE

Case Study

Mr T

- 6 year old Thoroughbred gelding.
- Single race preparation, trialled once, then retired from racing.
- Put in paddock 12 months after retirement, then spent 10 months with Thoroughbred rehoming association before going to current owner.
- Noted to have some postural issues, most likely due to poor conformation – low wither and neck. It was recognised that the horse needed to undertake a tailored training program to best prepare him for ridden work.

Transitioning a Thoroughbred from flat racing to a career as a performance horse is common, with some research showing an estimated 46% of racehorses retire to a performance career. The muscular and postural demands of disciplines like dressage and jumping differ from racing, necessitating appropriate strength and conditioning to prepare them for the change in career, and help prevent injury and enhance performance.

Common problems seen immediately after retirement in off-the-track Thoroughbreds (OTTBs) include increased thoracic lordosis (extension or 'dip' of the spinal posture), poor muscle development of back muscles and asymmetry of the muscle size from left to right due to training and racing predominately in one direction.

Before starting any ridden work, Mr T's owner arranged a saddle fitting assessment. He was observed to have an asymmetry of the muscles along the thoracic spine, along with poor topline and posture.

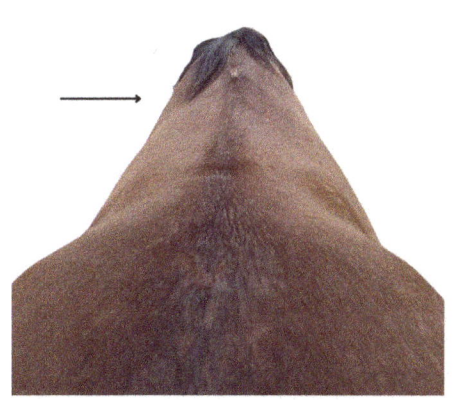
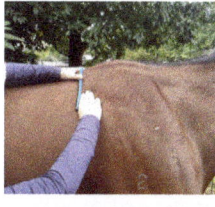
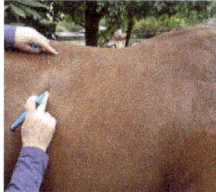

From left to right: 1. A top view of Mr T's back, in which you can see the muscular wastage on the left as indicated by the arrow.
2. and 3. The saddle fitter measured symmetry and back posture to provide a benchmark and to ensure the saddle fit would be correct for his back shape.

TOPLINE & POSTURE

Mr T was noted to stand with a slightly extended spinal posture, i.e., a dipped back posture. He had an "upside down" neck, with a notable dip in front of the wither and poor muscle development along the top of the neck, with prominent underside muscle development. Overall, he had poor general muscular development of the spinal and hindquarter muscles.

A nutritional analysis was undertaken using a horse nutrition calculator and an increase in roughage (hay) was recommended to be added to his diet, along with high-quality protein following exercise.

Exercise choice and prescription

The owner, in collaboration with the veterinary professionals working with her, chose to work on a groundwork program as opposed to a ridden program for the following reasons:
- The saddle fitter advised they wanted to improve his muscular development and posture before fitting him for a new saddle. This would save time and money by reducing the need for repeated saddle adjustments, as it was predicted his posture and shape would change to the point that a saddle alteration would be required.
- Mr T lacked general muscle and strength. Groundwork training would allow him to build this strength and learn to balance himself before adding the extra load of a rider.

3-5 training sessions per week were performed, with the number of sessions per week dictated by factors such as the weather or the owner's other commitments. A minimum of three sessions were performed each week, for 20-30 minutes each. Mr T lived out in a paddock with other horses 24/7.

Which exercises were performed and why

- Groundwork exercises, including leg yield, back in hand and tight turns. This was done both in the arena and when out walking out on the road/trails. More repetitions were completed to Mr T's weaker side (the left) to increase the load and intensity.
    - Leg yields were included to help improve straightness and suppleness, as well as improving strength and balance.
    - Tight turns were included to help improve lateral bend suppleness and stability, along with thoracic sling and hindquarter strength.
    - Backing in-hand was used to encourage Mr T to lift through the shoulders by engaging the thoracic sling and transfer more weight to the hindquarters.

TOPLINE & POSTURE

- Long lining – straight lines, loops, change of direction, serpentines, circles and weaves. Long lining is useful to condition the walk or trot without the weight or influence of the rider. It was included to help improve straightness, symmetry and suppleness.

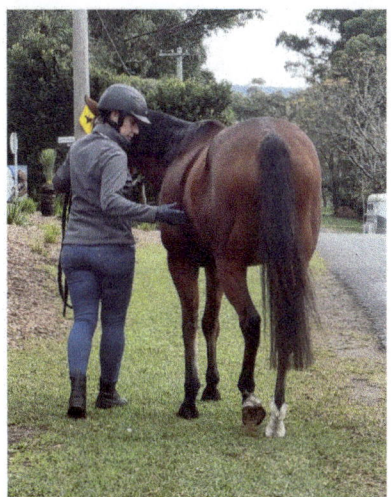

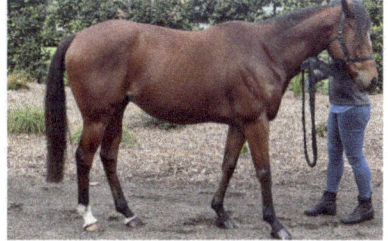

From left to right: 1. performing leg yield in hand whilst out on a road walk, 2. long lining wide weave exercise and 3. backing in-hand.

- Lunge – walk, trot and canter were performed on the lunge under the following conditions:
  - One loose side rein – Mr T had a tendency to twist his head to the left on the lunge on a left circle, making it difficult to get him to work evenly. Placing just one side rein (very loosely so that he could still stretch his nose forward) on the outside when lunging to the left encouraged him to be straighter and work more effectively, as the side rein plus inside lunge rein equated to two reins.
  - Cavesson – lunging with a cavesson helps build suppleness, strength of the hindquarters and lifting of the thoracic sling and back, helping to improve posture. In a cavesson, the lunge attaches to the front of the nose, rather than the bit. This typically allows the handler to have greater control of neck flexion and lateral bend.
  - Poles – poles were placed on a circle, either as a single pole or a fan configuration, and Mr T was asked to walk or trot over the poles. This added an additional abdominal and thoracic sling strengthening element to the exercise.
  - Transitions – lots of transitions were performed in all gaits, from halt, walk, trot and canter. Transitions are useful to improve engagement and strength of the hindquarter, spine and thoracic sling musculature, as well as whole body posture, balance and control.

TOPLINE & POSTURE

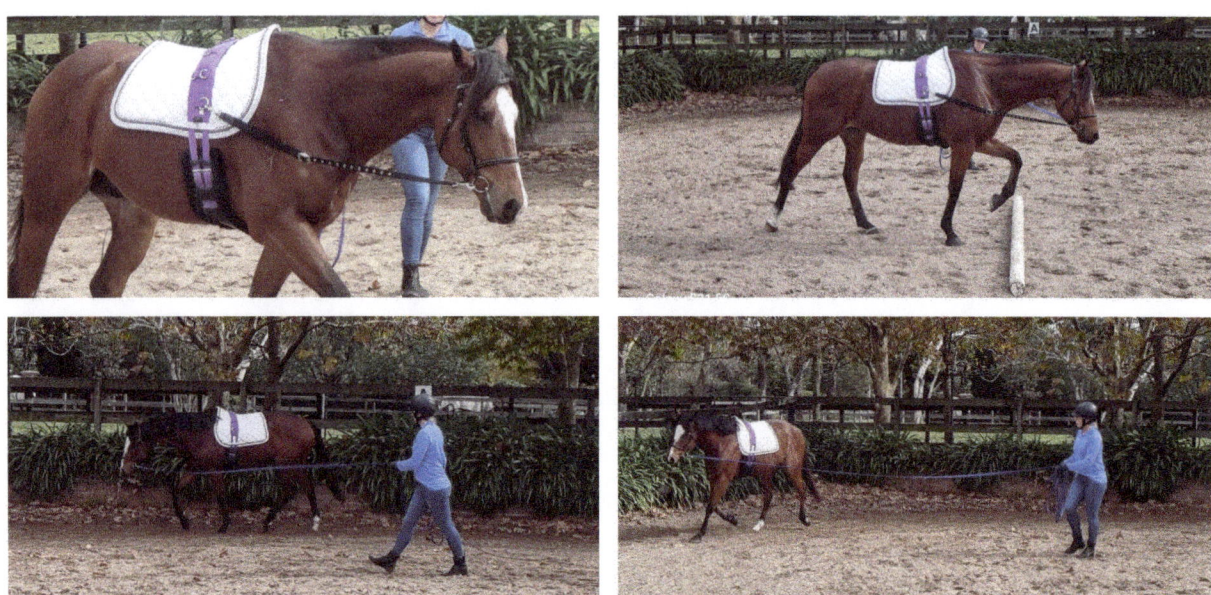

From left to right: 1. an outside side rein being used to help keep Mr T more balanced on the lunge. Note that it is kept loose to allow him to still stretch his nose forward and down. 2. Combining pole work and lunging. 3 and 4. Moving between walk and trot transitions on the lunge.

- Walk and trot in-hand – it's important to not underestimate the benefits of walking and trotting out on different surfaces and terrain. This was added to Mr T's program both for the physical benefits but also for the mental stimulation it can provide.
    - Encouraging a head low position and a forward active walk, moving between different surfaces and gradients. This not only helps improve strength and posture but also proprioception.
    - Walk and trot up/down hill – working uphill particularly helps strengthen the hindquarters, neck and back muscles, while in negotiating downhill Mr T had to rely heavily on eccentric (slow, controlled) muscular contractions, particularly of the forelimb, potentially making it a useful exercise to help strengthen the thoracic sling.

TOPLINE & POSTURE

Sample weekly training plan

Monday
1. In-hand session out on road and trail 25 minutes
   a. Leg yield along the edge of track 5 metres x 5 each direction
   b. Tight turns x 6 each direction
   c. Forward active walk 15 minutes, variety of surfaces and gradients
   d. Trot 3 x 1.5 minutes, variety of surfaces and gradients

Tuesday
Rest

Wednesday
1. Lunge session 20 minutes, focusing on transitions between halt, walk and trot

Thursday
1. Long lining session 20 minutes, including:
   a. Wide weaves x 3 each direction
   b. Shallow weaves x 3 each direction
   c. Change rein across diagonal x 5 each rein
   d. 2 loops along long side x 3 each rein

Friday
Rest

Saturday
1. In-hand session out on road and trail 25 minutes
   a. Leg yield along the edge of track 5 metres x 5 each direction
   b. Tight turns x 6 each direction
   c. Forward active walk 15 minutes, variety of surfaces and gradients
   d. Trot 3 x 1.5 minutes, variety of surfaces and gradients

Sunday
1. Pole session 10 minutes:
   a. Single raised pole walk in-hand on flat x 5 reps and incline x 5 reps
   b. Single raised pole trot in-hand on flat x 6 reps
   c. Maze walk in-hand x 5 reps each direction

TOPLINE & POSTURE

After 8 weeks of groundwork training, Mr T showed noticeable improvement in muscle development, topline and posture. A repeat saddle fit assessment revealed improved symmetry along his back, allowing a saddle to be fitted that would be more balanced and comfortable for Mr T.

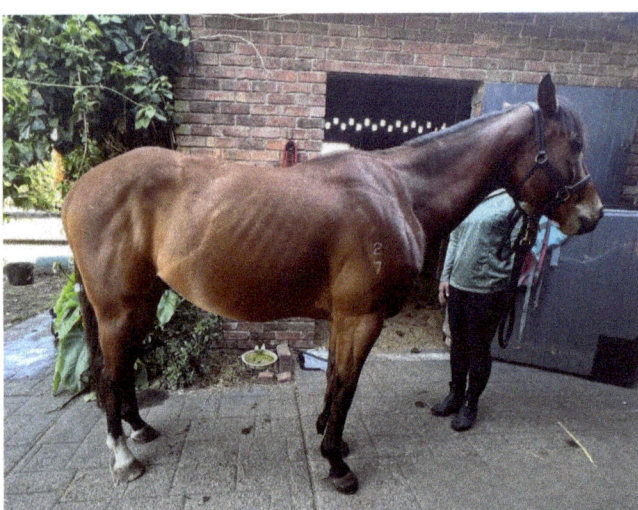 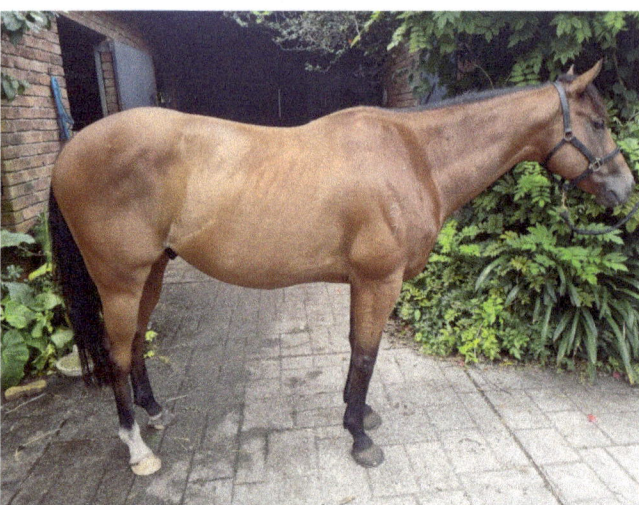

A comparison of Mr T at the beginning of the program (left) and at the end of the 8 weeks (right). Please note that these photos are not ideal, as they are taken from a different position and distance from the horse. We've included them here only to highlight the basic differences in his condition and posture.

SADDLE FIT

It is beyond the scope of this book, and our qualifications, to fully cover the topic of saddle fitting. However, in our years of practice as physiotherapists, we have worked with many saddle fitters and treated countless horses with back pain directly related to poorly fitting saddles. We regularly check the basics of saddle fit (and teach our clients how to do the same), so we know when we need to refer on to a qualified saddle fitter.

Having a basic understanding of how to recognise when your saddle doesn't fit correctly, or may be causing your horse pain, can save you significant money on veterinary, physiotherapy, or bodywork bills. It can also prevent years of lost progress due to poor performance, lost income if your horse works professionally, and even a trip to the emergency department (as Kristin can personally attest – read her story later in this chapter).

In this chapter, we cover many of the common signs your horse may display if they are experiencing back pain. Poor saddle fit can result in back pain, so should be considered a possible contributor whenever any of these behavioural signs are seen.

Some additional signs of poor saddle fit include:

- Horse reacting negatively when you brush or scrape the area of their back directly underneath where the saddle fits. Signs may include biting, dipping or flinching excessively through the back, or kicking out.
- Loss of muscle bulk under the saddle panel regions. This will often be particularly noticeable in the area just behind the wither.
- Uneven sweat patterns after riding, on either the horse or the saddle pad. Check your saddle pad routinely after a ride. If one section of the saddle pad is dry while everywhere else has sweat patches, this is a good indication that your saddle is not sitting evenly on the horse.
- White hairs or rub marks in any area underneath the saddle.
- Areas of swelling along the back after exercise.

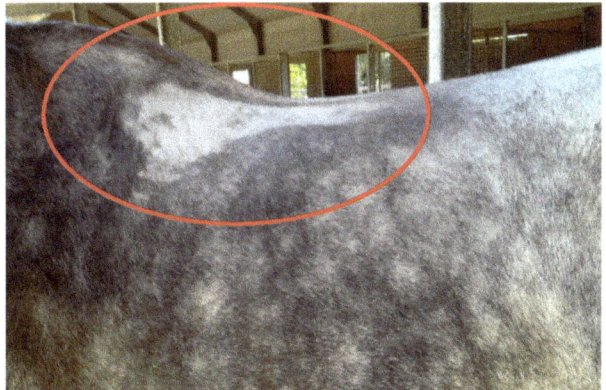 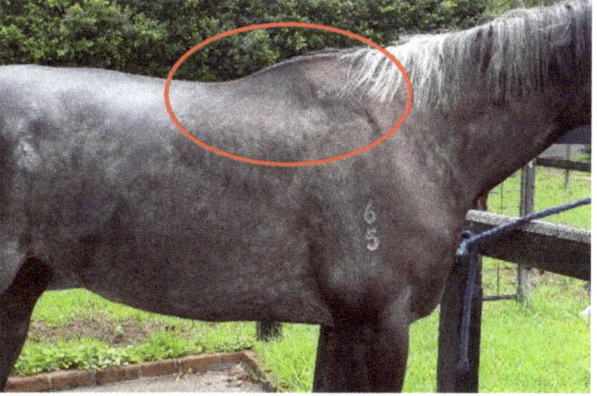

Dry patch underneath the saddle (left). Muscle atrophy (wasting) of the muscles running alongside and just behind the wither (right).

SADDLE FIT

How to check your saddle

It's imperative that you always have saddles fitted and checked by a qualified saddle fitter. This should be done at least once per year, and more frequently if your horse's body has changed shape or is showing any signs of back pain or discomfort. In between visits it's important to know how to check the basics, so that you know when to seek help:

- In an English style saddle, the saddle tree should not extend past the last rib (T18). To find this point, feel along the horse's ribs towards the hindquarters until you come to the last rib. Follow this rib along its length up towards the spine. The saddle should not extend further back than this point.
- The saddle should sit level on the horse's back. While symmetrical and slight movement from side to side is normal, it shouldn't slip more to one side, excessively lift at the back or shift forwards or backwards while the horse is moving.
- Ensure at least 2-3 fingers (about 3 cm) fit under the pommel (front of the saddle) with the rider standing in the stirrups.
- The gullet, which is the central channel on the underside of the saddle, should sit clear over the horse's spine. Standing next to the horse's shoulder, look through the front of the saddle towards the hindquarters. You should be able to see through the gullet, noting if there is any contact with it on the horse's spine.
- The panels on the underside of the saddle should be smooth and make even contact with the horse's back, without gaps or pressure points. When the saddle is off, regularly run your hands along the panels to feel for any unevenness in the flocking.
- With the saddle on and the girth secured, check the contact by sliding your hand under the panels. Ideally, there should be consistent contact along the entire length of each panel. Sometimes, the front and back make contact while the middle does not – this is called bridging. If you find areas with little or no contact, or spots where it's very hard to slide your hand under the panel, this indicates an issue with the fit. In these cases, it's important to have your saddle professionally assessed and adjusted.

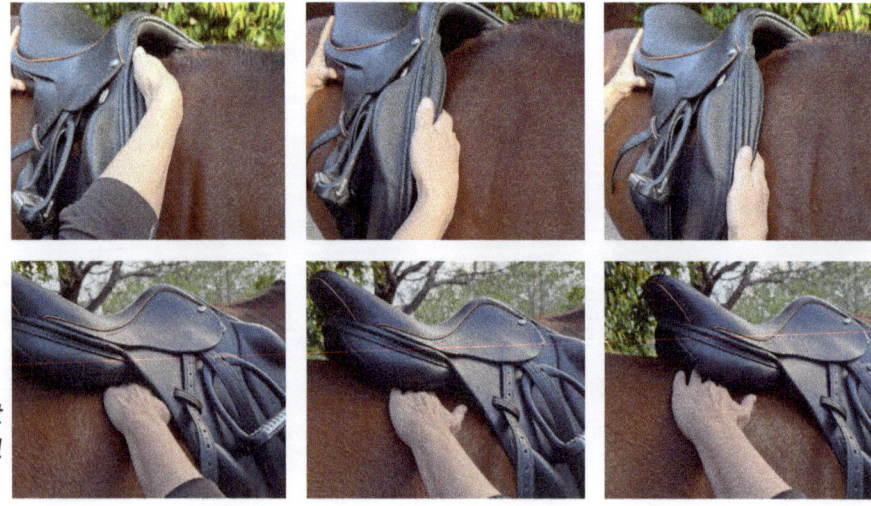

Assessing contact of the front panel (top) and back panel (bottom).

SADDLE FIT

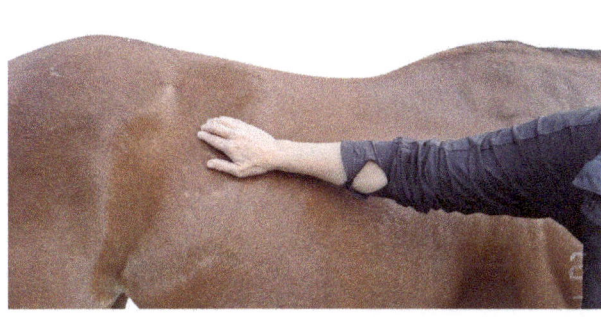 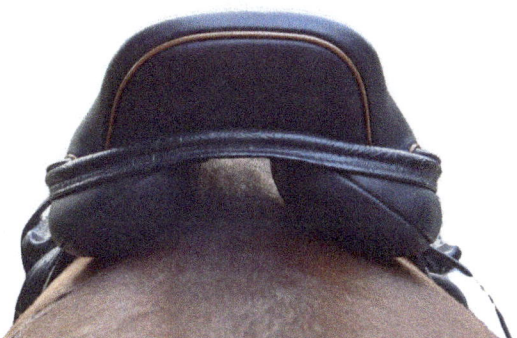

Location of the last rib (18) left. From the back or front, check for gullet clearance and ensure that both back panels are in contact with the back (right).

If you're ever unsure, it's best to seek advice from a trained professional. A thorough saddle fit will include standing assessment, as well as ridden, to ensure a correct fit. It's essential that the saddle fits both horse and rider. A seat size or shape that doesn't suit the rider's pelvis and leg length makes it difficult to sit evenly and balanced. A rider struggling to maintain a balanced position in the saddle may shift their weight unevenly, creating increased areas of pressure under the saddle which can contribute to soreness and poor performance.

 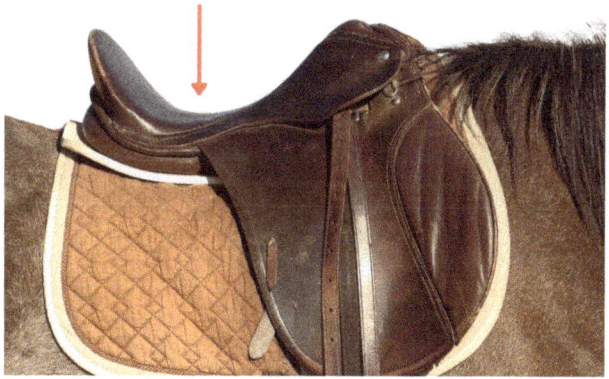

Saddle with a balanced pitch with the lowest flat point located in the middle of the saddle (left). Saddle with a backwards pitch, with the lowest flat point located well back in the saddle (right). This will create extra pressure underneath the back of the saddle, and make it very difficult for the rider to sit balanced on the horse.

BACK PAIN IN THE HORSE

Back pain is a common problem in both sport and racehorses, and can present in many different ways. Research suggests that up to 94% of ridden horses experience back pain at some point in their careers, yet it is often overlooked as a cause of poor performance or behavioural issues by many people. Being able to recognise when your horse is showing signs of pain or discomfort in the back is crucial for catching problems early and keeping your horse, yourself, and others safe.

Kristin's story

I learnt this the hard way. As a fairly green horse owner at the age of 20, I had been riding for 10 years so thought I knew a lot, but now recognise that there was so much I didn't know or understand about horses. I don't recall learning about saddle fit at pony or riding club in the 1990s, and none of my coaches over the years ever mentioned it. When I got a new horse, I simply used the saddle I had been riding my other horse in, without any thought about whether it might fit him properly. I rode in this saddle for about a year with no apparent issue, at least, none that I recognised (which in hindsight isn't saying much!)

One day I went for a routine ride, getting on as usual at the mounting block and walking 20 metres to the arena. Just as I was about to enter, my horse started to buck. I'm not talking one or two half-hearted bucks, but a good 20 seconds of serious broncing.

Naturally, I fell off and smashed the bone right at my elbow joint into several pieces, requiring surgery and a long, painful rehabilitation. This prompted me to investigate what had caused the episode, as it was very out of character for my horse and, at the time, seemed to come completely out of the blue. I was in my first year at university studying human physiotherapy, and based on what I was starting to learn, and on the advice of my vet, I had both a physio and a saddle fitter look at my horse. They found that he was significantly sore through his back and that my saddle didn't fit him at all. Thankfully, after diligently following the physio's advice and getting a properly fitted new saddle, my horse improved and we never had a repeat of what was a distressing situation, no doubt for my horse as much as me.

What this taught me, and what I've seen time and again in my career as an equine physio, is that he had been telling me long before that day that something was wrong, and I didn't listen. Not because I didn't care, but because I didn't know what to listen for. Looking back now, some of these signs included poor hindlimb propulsion with a short stepping hindlimb gait and difficulties with transitions that became quite significant just before my fall.

BACK PAIN IN THE HORSE

When we're learning to ride, we're often told to "kick him on," "don't let her do that," or "he's just trying it on." We're actively taught not to listen to our horses, but instead to dominate them and make them do what we want.

I strongly believe that no horse is inherently naughty. My horse didn't just decide that he was going to play up that day. Horses react to their environment and how they feel. On that day, he needed whatever was causing him pain to stop, by whatever means necessary.

Signs of back pain

Kristin's horse had been expressing signs of pain in more subtle ways before that day. Some of the common signs your horse may be communicating that their back is troubling them are listed below. These have been reported in studies where horse owners recorded the behaviours of their horses with clinically diagnosed back pain. Some of these will be obvious, but others can be more subtle or discounted as training or behavioural issues. This list is in no way exhaustive, and may indicate problems other than back pain. Recognising any of these signs in your horse can indicate that something is wrong. It always warrants further investigation with your vet as your first step.

Ground behaviours (when handled or observed)
- Unwillingness to stand still
- Disliking being brushed or scraped over the back
- Teeth grinding
- Aggressive behaviour (towards people or other horses)
- Change in posture (e.g., standing camped under or with an extended/dipped back posture)
- Heat felt over the back
- Shifting weight constantly behind
- Kicking out during handling or grooming
- Loss of topline muscle
- Tail swishing during grooming or saddling
- Depressed or tense demeanour
- Girthiness

Many of these behaviours can be related to other issues. Girthiness, in particular, can be caused by intestinal/stomach issues (such as ulcers), pain through the pectorals or poor girth and/or saddle fit. Compared to some of the other behaviours listed above, girthiness is commonly disregarded as poor behaviour, or something the horse has "always done". Like all of the behaviours listed above, it's not normal, and should always be investigated.

BACK PAIN IN THE HORSE

Ridden behaviours
- Bucking / rearing
- Bunny hopping gait in the hindlimbs
- Difficulty in transitions (e.g., trot to canter)
- Hindlimb lameness
- Forelimb lameness
- Difficulty sliding/stopping (especially in Western disciplines)
- Unwilling to go forward under saddle
- Difficulty holding canter leads
- Loss of impulsion
- Refusing jumps
- Missing lead changes
- Hollowing through the back/coming above the vertical
- Overflexing the neck to avoid using the back
- Excessive head tossing
- Reluctance to turn or bend
- Opening the mouth/showing teeth
- Uneven rein contact
- Tripping
- Bracing through the body
- Short stepping gait, especially in the hindlimbs

Some behaviours your horse will show under saddle if their back is sore can be obvious, such as bucking or refusing a jump (left and centre). Some, however, can be more subtle, such as being overbent through the neck or repeatedly opening and closing their mouth and/or exposing their teeth (right).

Behaviours may stem from pain or training issues, but pain should always be considered and addressed first before evaluating training. If you are noticing a combination of any of these behaviours occurring repeatedly, please seek veterinary advice.

RECOGNISING BACK PAIN

Case Study

Ms A

- 13 year old Quarter Horse mare.
- Competing in regular reining competitions, and training 5 days a week.
- Owner has noticed recently that performance has dropped off and that she seems less willing in her work.

We often assume that if a horse is suffering from back pain, it will be quite obvious to us. In actual fact, the signs that our horses show us can be quite subtle or easily considered to be a training issue. Kissing spines, also known as impinging or overriding dorsal spinous processes, is a condition where the spinous processes of the vertebrae touch or overlap. It is a common condition and cause of back pain, although many horses show either no or only very subtle signs of pain or discomfort.

Ms A is an example of a horse only showing quite subtle signs. The main issues that were observed related to her training and performance. Some of the changes Ms A displayed under saddle that highlighted a problem to the owner included:

- Placing her ears back every time the saddle was placed on her back and girth done up.
- Difficulty with lead changes, becoming what the owner described as "sticky", with the hindlimbs lagging and not engaging in the changes.
- Spins became very stiff to the right and sliding stops started to lose their usual power, with Ms A seeming resistant to perform the movement.

Recognising that this was not common behaviour for his horse, Ms A's owner decided to seek veterinary advice rather than pushing her through. On examination, the vet observed that Ms A appeared to have some soreness on palpation of her spine. An x-ray confirmed the presence of mild kissing spines in the thoracic region. This diagnosis was confirmed as a source of pain with local anaesthesia temporarily improving her symptoms.

With a tailored management and rehabilitation plan developed in conjunction with a physiotherapist, Ms A was able to return to work and competition comfortably.

Chapter 7

THE HORSE-RIDER RELATIONSHIP

Understanding how the rider can influence the horse's movement, posture and symmetry

CONSIDERING THE RIDER IN TRAINING

Impact of the rider on the horse's limbs

When a horse is ridden, it's not just a simple matter of them carrying extra weight. The horse actually changes how it moves. Research comparing how a horse trots with and without a rider found that, while the overall force on their legs increased with the rider, the forces were actually lower than expected when adjusted for the combined horse-and-rider weight. In other words, what they found is that horses actively change their movement patterns to manage the load of a rider, rather than just absorbing the extra weight. One of the key changes observed was increased extension (or drop) of the front fetlocks during the later part of the stride.

Understanding that a horse adapts its movement when ridden helps us make informed decisions about workload and injury prevention. If a horse is consistently ridden in a way that places extra demand on the forelimbs, like circles or extended strides, it may increase the risk of strain-related injuries over time. Remembering that a horse's forelimbs already show increased fetlock drop during increased speed, circles, and jumping, adding a rider further increases limb load, so training should be structured with this in mind. Balancing training with things like varied terrain, balancing high-intensity sessions with light/rest days, and performing groundwork to build strength and resilience (without the added weight of a rider) are all strategies that can be used.

Impact of the rider on the horse's back

One of the main goals of becoming a skilled rider is to be as easy a load as possible for your horse to carry. Studies have shown that a horse's back becomes more extended (i.e., dips) when carrying a saddle, and even more so when adding a rider, compared to moving without either. This increased extension occurs across all gaits.

Many riders believe that rising trot is easier on the horse's back than sitting trot. That's true to an extent, but perhaps not to the degree many expect. Research indicates that sitting trot results in greater overall back extension and a higher head and neck position when compared to trotting without a rider. In rising trot, the horse's back is more flexed during the "rise" phase, and more extended whenever the rider sits. So, while rising trot may appear to reduce force, the spine still extends just as much as it does in sitting trot, it simply doesn't stay extended throughout. This alternating pattern of flexion and extension may help improve spinal suppleness, but it also shows that rising trot can still place significant strain on the horse's back.

Rider position can influence both how stable the rider is and how much force is placed on the horse's back. In terms of front-to-back stability, the two-point seat (where the rider is slightly lifted out of the saddle, with weight more through the stirrups) offers the most rider stability. Next is the rising trot, and the least stable position is the sitting trot.

CONSIDERING THE RIDER IN TRAINING

When it comes to side-to-side stability, there's not much difference between these three positions. What does change significantly between positions is the amount of force transmitted to the horse's back. Research has shown that sitting trot produces the highest peak force (around 2112 N (Newtons)), followed by rising trot (2056 N), while the two-point seat produces the least (1688 N). While sitting and rising trot create similar levels of force, moving to a two-point seat results in a noticeably lower load on the horse's back.

Obviously, it's not practical to ride in a two-point seat all the time, but it's still really important to understand how your position affects your horse. When you can, try mixing things up during trot work. After a break or if your horse is coming back from an injury, riding in a two-point or light seat for a while can be a great way to ease them back into work, without putting as much strain on their back.

CHALLENGE

To help you think about the influence you have on the horse's back, set yourself the following challenge. For every ride you have during a 1-month period, spend at least 5 minutes in a "hover" position. To do this, stand up in the stirrups as your horse trots. Incline your trunk slightly forward to keep your centre of gravity (chest region) directly over your base of support (feet). You'll feel you are between a full two-point position and a light seat position. The benefits of doing this will include:

- Less force through your horse's back, which in turn will help your horse to be better able to flex through the spine and engage their abdominal, thoracic sling and back muscles, helping to strengthen their topline.
- Improve your lower leg position and strength. We use this exercise a lot with riders who struggle with keeping the lower leg underneath themselves and absorbing weight down through the knee and ankle. A great exercise for those who have a tendency to sit in an 'armchair' seat.

You can choose to do 5 mins all at once or break it up into smaller intervals. And you don't have to limit yourself to 5 mins, if you want to do longer, go for it!

CONSIDERING THE RIDER IN TRAINING

Impact of weight on movement and lameness

The total weight that a horse carries (which includes both rider and tack) can alter their movement. You've probably heard of the "20% rule" – that rider plus tack shouldn't exceed 20% of the horse's body weight. One study looked into how rider weight, the rider-to-horse weight ratio, and saddle fit affect how horses move and behave. They found that horses carrying higher total loads were more likely to show signs of discomfort or lameness, particularly in trot or canter or on tasks such as small circles or transitions.

To make your training more effective and comfortable for your horse, it helps to know the total weight you're asking your horse to carry. It's important to calculate total weight, not just weight of the rider.

Step 1 – Weigh the rider:
- Measure yourself wearing your usual riding clothes, boots and helmet.

Step 2 – Weigh your saddle and tack:
- Weigh your saddle separately, along with girth, saddle pads, bridle, and any other equipment you usually use.
- Add these together to get the total tack weight.

Step 3 – Calculate total load:
- Add your weight to your tack weight to give you the total load that your horse carries.

Step 4 – Compare to your horse's weight:
- Ideally, the total load should not exceed approximately 20% of your horse's body weight. If you don't know your horse's exact weight, you can use an online horse weight calculator or weight tape to determine it with relative accuracy.
- Use this information to plan training sessions, choose appropriate exercises, or to consider changes in tack or workload.

Even if your total load is under 20%, pay attention to how your horse responds under saddle. Saddle fit, rider balance, and skill are just as important as weight alone.

CONSIDERING THE RIDER IN TRAINING

Rider symmetry & fitness

One of the key considerations in equestrian sports is rider symmetry and fitness. It's a unique challenge because you're working with two athletes, horse and rider, who must function as a unified pair. Asymmetry in one inevitably affects the other. The reality is that neither horse nor rider are ever perfectly symmetrical, so the goal is to achieve functional symmetry – as close to balanced as possible. When a rider lacks symmetry, it can alter the horse's spinal movement and limb mechanics. Studies have shown that asymmetrical rider position in the saddle increases fetlock extension (drop) at the trot in both the forelimbs and hindlimbs, and alters the range of motion along the spine. A rider collapsing or leaning to one side can also increase pressure under certain areas of the saddle.

Many riders are now starting to address this by engaging in structured off-horse exercise to improve their symmetry, fitness, strength, and posture. Research has shown that riders who completed an eight-week off-horse exercise program experienced a significant reduction in left–right pressure asymmetry under the saddle and their horses showed an 8.4% increase in stride length. This suggests that improving rider symmetry with an off-horse exercise program, may help reduce uneven loading on the horse's back during riding, while also potentially leading to improved horse movement and performance.

Aerobic or cardiovascular endurance refers to how well the heart and lungs can deliver oxygen to the working muscles during prolonged exercise. There have been a handful of research studies to measure riders' heart rates during riding to indicate how intense a variety of ridden activities are. Heart rates generally increase with faster gaits and reach very high rates during activities requiring the rider to be in two-point seat (e.g., racing, polo, jumping, galloping). This is probably because these activities use significant leg muscle strength and require more trunk control. Jenni-Louise Douglas, at the University of Worcester, England, has researched the physiological demands of eventing. She found that a rider's heart rate in a cross-country phase of eventing can reach on average 85-95% of their maximal heart rate for 5+ minutes. These results are supported by testing of Australian elite dressage and eventing riders during competition, finding that during dressage tests, riders are usually working at about 80% of their maximum, and during cross-country greater than 90%. A rider with excellent aerobic endurance will be able to perform sustained exercise without fatiguing, giving them the ability to respond to sudden changes in conditions and to be more effective at making decisions quickly. Consider the effects of a tired rider on their horse – they may not be able to balance as well, be in sync with the horse's movement, or apply the aids as smoothly, resulting in poor performance or worse yet, risky situations. Building fitness off the horse can improve endurance, balance and overall riding effectiveness.

CONSIDERING THE RIDER IN TRAINING

Key Points

- Horses adapt their movement in order to carry a rider, which places extra load on the forelimbs. Be sure to factor this in when designing your training programs.
- The rider's position, particularly during trot, directly affects the forces on the horse's back. Using a lighter seat on occasion, such as a two-point or hover, and alternating between rising and sitting during a training session can help minimise load through the back.
- The combined weight of rider and tack affects a horse's movement. Knowing the total load and adjusting training or tack choice can help play a role in injury management.
- Undertaking an off-horse exercise program, particularly one that has been designed by a trained health or fitness professional, may help improve your symmetry in the saddle, reducing uneven pressure underneath the saddle and enhancing the horse's biomechanics and performance.
- Good aerobic fitness will assist in maintaining good posture and balance on your horse – lowering adverse effects of poor rider balance on the horse. Consider training at high aerobic intensities off the horse (consult a professional to set up an appropriate program for you).

Working on exercises, both on and off the horse, will be beneficial in improving rider symmetry and strength, ultimately leading to enhanced horse and rider performance.

REFERENCE LIST

Hoof
- Leśniak, K., Williams, J., Kuznik, K., & Douglas, P. (2017). Does a 4-6 Week Shoeing Interval Promote Optimal Foot Balance in the Working Equine?. Animals : an open access journal from MDPI, 7(4), 29. https://doi.org/10.3390/ani7040029
- Mata, F., Franca, I., Araújo, J., Paixão, G., Lesniak, K., & Cerqueira, J. L. (2024). Investigating Associations between Horse Hoof Conformation and Presence of Lameness. Animals : an open access journal from MDPI, 14(18), 2697. https://doi.org/10.3390/ani14182697
- Sharp, Y., & Tabor, G. (2022). An Investigation into the Effects of Changing Dorso-Plantar Hoof Balance on Equine Hind Limb Posture. Animals : an open access journal from MDPI, 12(23), 3275. https://doi.org/10.3390/ani12233275
- Hobbs, S. J., Nauwelaerts, S., Sinclair, J., Clayton, H. M., & Back, W. (2018). Sagittal plane fore hoof unevenness is associated with fore and hindlimb asymmetrical force vectors in the sagittal and frontal planes. PloS one, 13(8), e0203134. https://doi.org/10.1371/journal.pone.0203134

Aerobic Fitness
- Rietmann, T. R., Stauffacher, M., Bernasconi, P., Auer, J. A., & Weishaupt, M. A. (2004). The association between heart rate, heart rate variability, endocrine and behavioural pain measures in horses suffering from laminitis. Journal of veterinary medicine. A, Physiology, pathology, clinical medicine, 51(5), 218–225. https://doi.org/10.1111/j.1439-0442.2004.00627.x
- Kapteijn, C. M., Frippiat, T., van Beckhoven, C., van Lith, H. A., Endenburg, N., Vermetten, E., & Rodenburg, T. B. (2022). Measuring heart rate variability using a heart rate monitor in horses (Equus caballus) during groundwork. Frontiers in veterinary science, 9, 939534. https://doi.org/10.3389/fvets.2022.939534
- Ter Woort, F., Dubois, G., Tansley, G., Didier, M., Verdegaal, L., Franklin, S., & Van Erck-Westergren, E. (2022). Validation of an equine fitness tracker: ECG quality and arrhythmia detection. Equine veterinary journal, 55(2), 336–343. Advance online publication. https://doi.org/10.1111/evj.13565
- Bitschnaul, C., Jones, J., Haldi, J., Laukkanen, R. & Weishaupt, W. (2013) White Paper – Polar Sport Zones for horses.

Interval Training
- Mukai, K., Ohmura, H., Takahashi, Y., Ebisuda, Y., Yoneda, K., & Miyata, H. (2023). Physiological and skeletal muscle responses to high-intensity interval exercise in Thoroughbred horses. Frontiers in veterinary science, 10, 1241266. https://doi.org/10.3389/fvets.2023.1241266

Strength Training
- Rhea, M. R., Alvar, B. A., Burkett, L. N., & Ball, S. D. (2003). A meta-analysis to determine the dose response for strength development. Medicine and science in sports and exercise, 35(3), 456–464. https://doi.org/10.1249/01.MSS.0000053727.63505.D4

Mobility & Stretching
- Thomas, E., Bianco, A., Paoli, A., & Palma, A. (2018). The Relation Between Stretching Typology and Stretching Duration: The Effects on Range of Motion. International journal of sports medicine, 39(4), 243–254. https://doi.org/10.1055/s-0044-101146
- Rose, N. S., Northrop, A. J., Brigden, C. V., & Martin, J. H. (2009). Effects of a stretching regime on stride length and range of motion in equine trot. Veterinary journal (London, England : 1997), 181(1), 53–55. https://doi.org/10.1016/j.tvjl.2009.03.010

REFERENCE LIST

- Morton, S. K., Whitehead, J. R., Brinkert, R. H., & Caine, D. J. (2011). Resistance training vs. static stretching: effects on flexibility and strength. Journal of strength and conditioning research, 25(12), 3391–3398. https://doi.org/10.1519/JSC.0b013e31821624aa
- Alizadeh, S., Daneshjoo, A., Zahiri, A., Anvar, S. H., Goudini, R., Hicks, J. P., Konrad, A., & Behm, D. G. (2023). Resistance Training Induces Improvements in Range of Motion: A Systematic Review and Meta-Analysis. Sports medicine (Auckland, N.Z.), 53(3), 707–722. https://doi.org/10.1007/s40279-022-01804-x
- Rosenfeldt, M., Stien, N., Behm, D. G., Saeterbakken, A. H., & Andersen, V. (2024). Comparison of resistance training vs static stretching on flexibility and maximal strength in healthy physically active adults, a randomized controlled trial. BMC sports science, medicine & rehabilitation, 16(1), 142. https://doi.org/10.1186/s13102-024-00934-1
- Behm, D. G., Blazevich, A. J., Kay, A. D., & McHugh, M. (2016). Acute effects of muscle stretching on physical performance, range of motion, and injury incidence in healthy active individuals: a systematic review. Applied physiology, nutrition, and metabolism = Physiologie appliquee, nutrition et metabolisme, 41(1), 1–11. https://doi.org/10.1139/apnm-2015-0235
- McHugh, M. P., & Nesse, M. (2008). Effect of stretching on strength loss and pain after eccentric exercise. Medicine and science in sports and exercise, 40(3), 566–573.
- Trajano, G. S., Nosaka, K., & Blazevich, A. J. (2017). Neurophysiological Mechanisms Underpinning Stretch-Induced Force Loss. Sports medicine (Auckland, N.Z.), 47(8), 1531–1541. https://doi.org/10.1007/s40279-017-0682-6
- Konrad, A., Reiner, M. M., Thaller, S., & Tilp, M. (2019). The time course of muscle-tendon properties and function responses of a five-minute static stretching exercise. European journal of sport science, 19(9), 1195–1203. https://doi.org/10.1080/17461391.2019.1580319
- Palmer, T. B., Pineda, J. G., Cruz, M. R., & Agu-Udemba, C. C. (2019). Duration-Dependent Effects of Passive Static Stretching on Musculotendinous Stiffness and Maximal and Rapid Torque and Surface Electromyography Characteristics of the Hamstrings. Journal of strength and conditioning research, 33(3), 717–726. https://doi.org/10.1519/JSC.0000000000003031
- Kay, A. D., Husbands-Beasley, J., & Blazevich, A. J. (2015). Effects of Contract-Relax, Static Stretching, and Isometric Contractions on Muscle-Tendon Mechanics. Medicine and science in sports and exercise, 47(10), 2181–2190. https://doi.org/10.1249/MSS.0000000000000632
- Pethick, J., Moran, J., & Behm, D. G. (2023). Prolonged static stretching increases the magnitude and decreases the complexity of knee extensor muscle force fluctuations. PloS one, 18(7), e0288167. https://doi.org/10.1371/journal.pone.0288167
- Opplert, J., & Babault, N. (2018). Acute Effects of Dynamic Stretching on Muscle Flexibility and Performance: An Analysis of the Current Literature. Sports medicine (Auckland, N.Z.), 48(2), 299–325. https://doi.org/10.1007/s40279-017-0797-9
- Behm, D. G., Button, D. C., & Butt, J. C. (2001). Factors affecting force loss with prolonged stretching. Canadian journal of applied physiology = Revue canadienne de physiologie appliquee, 26(3), 261–272.
- Herman, S. L., & Smith, D. T. (2008). Four-week dynamic stretching warm-up intervention elicits longer-term performance benefits. Journal of strength and conditioning research, 22(4), 1286–1297. https://doi.org/10.1519/JSC.0b013e318173da50
- Malek, N. F. A., Nadzalan, A. M., Tan, K., Nor Azmi, A. M., Krishnan Vasanthi, R., Pavlović, R., Badau, D., & Badau, A. (2024). The Acute Effect of Dynamic vs. Proprioceptive Neuromuscular Facilitation Stretching on Sprint and Jump Performance. Journal of functional morphology and kinesiology, 9(1), 42. https://doi.org/10.3390/jfmk9010042

REFERENCE LIST

Rest & Recovery
- Minami, Y., Kawai, M., Migita, T. C., Hiraga, A., & Miyata, H. (2011). Free radical formation after intensive exercise in thoroughbred skeletal muscles. Journal of equine science, 22(2), 21–28. https://doi.org/10.1294/jes.22.21
- Raphael, Teixeira-Neto & Ferraz, Guilherme & Moscardini, A. & Balsamão, G. & Souza, J. & Queiroz-Neto, Antonio. (2008). Alterations in muscular enzymes of horses competing long-distance endurance. Arquivo Brasileiro De Medicina Veterinaria E Zootecnia - ARQ BRAS MED VET ZOOTEC. 60. 10.1590/S0102-09352008000300004.
- Grgic, J., Schoenfeld, B. J., Skrepnik, M., Davies, T. B., & Mikulic, P. (2018). Effects of rest interval duration in resistance training on measures of muscular strength: A systematic review. Sports Medicine, 48(1), 137-151. https://doi.org/10.1007/s40279-017-0788-x
- Haddad, F., & Adams, G. R. (2002). Acute cellular and molecular responses to resistance exercise. Journal of Applied Physiology, 93(1), 394-403. https://doi.org/10.1152/japplphysiol.01153.2001
- Radaelli, R., Bottaro, M., Wilhelm, E. N., Wagner, D. R., & Pinto, R. S. (2012). Time course of strength and echo intensity recovery after resistance exercise in women. Journal of strength and conditioning research, 26(9), 2577–2584. https://doi.org/10.1519/JSC.0b013e31823dae96
- Butudom, P., Axiak, S. M., Nielsen, B. D., Eberhart, S. W., & Schott, H. C., Jr (2003). Effect of varying initial drink volume on rehydration of horses. Physiology & Behavior, 79(2), 135–142. https://doi.org/10.1016/s0031-9384(03)00085-4

Protein
- Mowry, K. C., Thomson-Parker, T. L., Morales, C., Fikes, K. K., Stutts, K. J., Leatherwood, J. L., Anderson, M. J., Smith, R. X., & Suagee-Bedore, J. K. (2022). Effects of Crude Rice Bran Oil and a Flaxseed Oil Blend in Young Horses Engaged in a Training Program. Animals : an open access journal from MDPI, 12(21), 3006. https://doi.org/10.3390/ani12213006
- Cintineo, H. P., Arent, M. A., Antonio, J., & Arent, S. M. (2018). Effects of Protein Supplementation on Performance and Recovery in Resistance and Endurance Training. Frontiers in nutrition, 5, 83. https://doi.org/10.3389/fnut.2018.00083
- Schoenfeld, B.J., Aragon, A.A. & Krieger, J.W. The effect of protein timing on muscle strength and hypertrophy: a meta-analysis. J Int Soc Sports Nutr 10, 53 (2013). https://doi.org/10.1186/1550-2783-10-53

Detraining
- Tyler, C. M., Golland, L. C., Evans, D. L., Hodgson, D. R., & Rose, R. J. (1998). Skeletal muscle adaptations to prolonged training, overtraining and detraining in horses. Pflugers Archiv, 436(3), 391-397. https://doi.org/10.1007/s004240050648
- Stellmack, J. M., Logan, A. A., Higgins, A. H., & Hoffman, R. M. (2024). Physiological comparison of conditioned and non-conditioned university horses following semester break. Journal of equine veterinary science, 140, 105143. https://doi.org/10.1016/j.jevs.2024.105143

Acute:Chronic Workload
- Maupin, D., Schram, B., Canetti, E., & Orr, R. (2020). The Relationship Between Acute: Chronic Workload Ratios and Injury Risk in Sports: A Systematic Review. Open access journal of sports medicine, 11, 51–75. https://doi.org/10.2147/OAJSM.S231405

REFERENCE LIST

- Munsters, C. C. B. M., Kingma, B. R. M., van den Broek, J., & Sloet van Oldruitenborgh-Oosterbaan, M. M. (2020). A prospective cohort study on the acute:chronic workload ratio in relation to injuries in high level eventing horses: A comprehensive 3-year study. Preventive veterinary medicine, 179, 105010. https://doi.org/10.1016/j.prevetmed.2020.105010

Pain
- Dalla Costa, E., Minero, M., Lebelt, D., Stucke, D., Canali, E., & Leach, M. C. (2014). Development of the Horse Grimace Scale (HGS) as a pain assessment tool in horses undergoing routine castration. PLoS One, 9(3), e92281. https://doi.org/10.1371/journal.pone.0092281
- Gleerup, K. B., Forkman, B., Lindegaard, C., & Andersen, P. H. (2015). An equine pain face. Veterinary Anaesthesia and Analgesia, 42(1), 103-114. https://doi.org/10.1111/vaa.12212
- Dyson, S., Berger, J. M., Ellis, A. D., & Mullard, J. (2018). Development of an ethogram for a pain scoring system in ridden horses and its application to determine the presence of musculoskeletal pain. Journal of Veterinary Behavior: Clinical Applications and Research, 23, 47–57.
- Dyson, S. (2022). The Ridden Horse Pain Ethogram. Equine Veterinary Education, 34, 372-380. https://doi.org/10.1111/eve.13468
- van Loon, J. P. A. M., & Macri, L. (2021). Objective Assessment of Chronic Pain in Horses Using the Horse Chronic Pain Scale (HCPS): A Scale-Construction Study. Animals (Basel), 11(6), 1826. https://doi.org/10.3390/ani11061826
- Auer, U., Kelemen, Z., Vogl, C., von Ritgen, S., Haddad, R., Torres Borda, L., Gabmaier, C., Breteler, J., & Jenner, F. (2024). Development, refinement, and validation of an equine musculoskeletal pain scale. Frontiers in pain research (Lausanne, Switzerland), 4, 1292299. https://doi.org/10.3389/fpain.2023.1292299
- Dalla Costa, E., Bracci, D., Dai, F., Lebelt, D., & Minero, M. (2017). Do different emotional states affect the Horse Grimace Scale score? A pilot study. Journal of Equine Veterinary Science, 54, 114-117. https://doi.org/10.1016/j.jevs.2017.03.221

Dynamic Mobilisation Exercises
- Stubbs NC, Kaiser LJ, Hauptman J, Clayton HM. Dynamic mobilisation exercises increase cross sectional area of musculus multifidus. Equine Vet J. 2011 Sep;43(5):522-9. doi: 10.1111/j.2042-3306.2010.00322.x. Epub 2011 Mar 15. PMID: 21496085.
- Tabor, G. (2015). The effect of dynamic mobilisation exercises on the equine multifidus muscle and thoracic profile. [Master's Thesis, Plymouth University]. https://pearl.plymouth.ac.uk/bitstream/handle/10026.1/3320/2015tabor10366547resM.pdf?sequence=1&isAllowed=y
- Coll, Judit & Blake, Scott & Blake, Roberta. (2023). Surface electromyography (sEMG) of equine core muscles and kinematics of lumbosacral joint during core strengthening exercises. 10.1101/2023.08.11.552791

Poles
- Shaw, K., Ursini, T., Levine, D., Richards, J., & Adair, S. (2021). The Effect of Ground Poles and Elastic Resistance Bands on Longissimus Dorsi and Rectus Abdominus Muscle Activity During Equine Walk and Trot. Journal of equine veterinary science, 107, 103772. https://doi.org/10.1016/j.jevs.2021.103772
- Ursini, T., Shaw, K., Levine, D., Richards, J., & Adair, H. S. (2022). Electromyography of the Multifidus Muscle in Horses Trotting During Therapeutic Exercises. Frontiers in veterinary science, 9, 844776. https://doi.org/10.3389/fvets.2022.844776

REFERENCE LIST

- Walker, V. A., Tranquillle, C. A., MacKechnie-Guire, R., Spear, J., Newton, R., & Murray, R. C. (2022). Effect of Ground and Raised Poles on Kinematics of the Walk. Journal of Equine Veterinary Science, 115, 104005. https://doi.org/10.1016/j.jevs.2022.104005
- Clayton, H. M., Stubbs, N. C., & Lavagnino, M. (2015). Stance phase kinematics and kinetics of horses trotting over poles. Equine Veterinary Journal, 47(1), 113–118. https://doi.org/10.1111/evj.12251

Gradients
- Sloet van Oldruitenborgh-Ooste, Barneveld A, Schamhardt HC. Effects of treadmill inclination on kinematics of the trot in Dutch Warmblood horses. Equine Vet J Suppl. 1997 May;(23):71-5. doi: 10.1111/j.2042-3306.1997.tb05058.x. PMID: 9354294.
- Hoyt, D. F., Molinari, M., Wickler, S. J., & Cogger, E. A. (2002). Effect of trotting speed, load and incline on hindlimb stance-phase kinematics. Equine Veterinary Journal Supplement, 34, 330-336. https://doi.org/10.1111/j.2042-3306.2002.tb05442.x
- Crook, T. C., Wilson, A., & Hodson-Tole, E. (2010). The effect of treadmill speed and gradient on equine hindlimb muscle activity. Equine Veterinary Journal Supplement, 38, 412-416. https://doi.org/10.1111/j.2042-3306.2010.00222.x
- Dutto, D. J., Hoyt, D. F., Cogger, E. A., & Wickler, S. J. (2004). Ground reaction forces in horses trotting up an incline and on the level over a range of speeds. Journal of Experimental Biology, 207(Pt 20), 3507-3514. https://doi.org/10.1242/jeb.01171

Surface
- Rohlf, C. M., Garcia, T. C., Fyhrie, D. P., le Jeune, S. S., Peterson, M. L., & Stover, S. M. (2023). Shear ground reaction force variation among equine arena surfaces. Veterinary Journal (London, England : 1997), 291, 105930. https://doi.org/10.1016/j.tvjl.2022.105930
- Holt, D., Northrop, A., Owen, A., Martin, J. H., & Hobbs, S. J. (2014). Use of surface testing devices to identify potential risk factors for synthetic equestrian surfaces. Procedia Engineering, 72, 949-954. https://doi.org/10.1016/j.proeng.2014.06.160

Speed - Trot
- Clayton H. M. (1994). Comparison of the stride kinematics of the collected, working, medium and extended trot in horses. Equine Veterinary jJournal, 26(3), 230–234. https://doi.org/10.1111/j.2042-3306.1994.tb04375.x
- Clayton, H. M., Schamhardt, H. C., & Hobbs, S. J. (2017). Ground reaction forces of elite dressage horses in collected trot and passage. Veterinary journal (London, England : 1997), 221, 30–33. https://doi.org/10.1016/j.tvjl.2017.01.016
- Clayton, H. M., & Hobbs, S. J. (2017). An exploration of strategies used by dressage horses to control moments around the center of mass when performing passage. PeerJ, 5, e3866. https://doi.org/10.7717/peerj.3866
- Clayton, H. M., & Hobbs, S. J. (2019). A Review of Biomechanical Gait Classification with Reference to Collected Trot, Passage and Piaffe in Dressage Horses. Animals : an open access journal from MDPI, 9(10), 763. https://doi.org/10.3390/ani9100763
- Clayton, H. M., Hobbs, S. J., Rhodin, M., Hernlund, E., Peterson, M., Bos, R., & Bragança, F. S. (2025). Vertical Movement of Head, Withers, and Pelvis of High-Level Dressage Horses Trotting in Hand vs. Being Ridden. Animals : an open access journal from MDPI, 15(2), 241. https://doi.org/10.3390/ani15020241

REFERENCE LIST

- Hobbs, S. J., & Clayton, H. M. (2013). Sagittal plane ground reaction forces, centre of pressure and centre of mass in trotting horses. Veterinary journal (London, England : 1997), 198 Suppl 1, e14–e19. https://doi.org/10.1016/j.tvjl.2013.09.027
- Hobbs, S. J., Richards, J., & Clayton, H. M. (2014). The effect of centre of mass location on sagittal plane moments around the centre of mass in trotting horses. Journal of biomechanics, 47(6), 1278–1286. https://doi.org/10.1016/j.jbiomech.2014.02.024
- Hobbs, S. J., & Clayton, H. M. (2019). Collisional mechanics of the diagonal gaits of horses over a range of speeds. PeerJ, 7, e7689. https://doi.org/10.7717/peerj.7689
- Walker, V. A., Tranquille, C. A., Newton, J. R., Dyson, S. J., Brandham, J., Northrop, A. J., & Murray, R. C. (2017). Comparison of limb kinematics between collected and lengthened (medium/extended) trot in two groups of dressage horses on two different surfaces. Equine Veterinary Journal, 49(5), 673–680. https://doi.org/10.1111/evj.12661
- Walker, V. A., Walters, J. M., Griffith, L., & Murray, R. C. (2013). The effect of collection and extension on tarsal flexion and fetlock extension at trot. Equine Veterinary Journal, 45(2), 245–248. https://doi.org/10.1111/j.2042-3306.2012.00617.x

Circles
- Logan AA, Snyder AJ, Nielsen BD. Circle Diameter Impacts Stride Frequency and Forelimb Stance Duration at Various Gaits in Horses. Sensors. 2023; 23(9):4232. https://doi.org/10.3390/s23094232
- Crevier-Denoix, N., Munoz-Nates, F., Camus, M., Ravary-Plumioen, B., Denoix, J. M., Pourcelot, P., & Chateau, H. (2017). Comparison of peak vertical force and vertical impulse in the inside and outside hind limbs in horses circling on a soft surface, at trot and canter. Computer Methods in Biomechanics and Biomedical Engineering, 20(sup1), S51–S52. https://doi.org/10.1080/10255842.2017.1382856
- Tranquille, C. A., Walker, V. A., Hodgins, D., McEwen, J., Roberts, C., Harris, P., Cnockaert, R., Guire, R., & Murray, R. C. (2017). Quantification of warm-up patterns in elite showjumping horses over three consecutive days: A descriptive study. Comparative Exercise Physiology, 13(2), 53–61. https://doi.org/10.3920/cep170009

Neck and Back Posture
- Rhodin, M., Johnston, C., Holm, K. R., Wennerstrand, J., & Drevemo, S. (2005). The influence of head and neck position on kinematics of the back in riding horses at the walk and trot. Equine Veterinary Journal, 37(1), 7–11. https://doi.org/10.2746/0425164054406928
- Von Borstel, U. U., Duncan, I. J. H., Shoveller, A. K., Merkies, K., Keeling, L. J., & Millman, S. T. (2009). Impact of riding in a coercively obtained Rollkur posture on welfare and fear of performance horses. Applied Animal Behaviour Science, 116(2–4), 228–236. https://doi.org/10.1016/j.applanim.2008.10.001

Back Pain
- Crawford, K. L., Finnane, A., Greer, R. M., Phillips, C. J. C., Woldeyohannes, S. M., Perkins, N. R., & Ahern, B. J. (2021). Appraising the Welfare of Thoroughbred Racehorses in Training in Queensland, Australia: The Incidence, Risk Factors and Outcomes for Horses after Retirement from Racing. Animals : an open access journal from MDPI, 11(1), 142. https://doi.org/10.3390/ani11010142

REFERENCE LIST

- Marshall-Gibson, M. E., Durham, M. G., Seabaugh, K. A., Moorman, V. J., & Ferris, D. J. (2023). Survey of equine veterinarians regarding primary equine back pain in the United States. Frontiers in veterinary science, 10, 1224605. https://doi.org/10.3389/fvets.2023.1224605
- Tabor, G., Williams, J. M., & Marlin, D. (2022). Saddle related equine back pain, muscle condition and behaviour. Abstract from 11th International Conference on Equine Exercise Physiology, Uppsala, Sweden. https://doi.org/10.3920/cep2022.s1

Influence of the Rider
- Clayton, Hilary & Lanovaz, Joel & Schamhardt, H.C. & Van Wessum, Rob. (1999). Rider effects on ground reaction forces and fetlock kinematics at the trot. Equine Veterinary Journal. Supplement. 30. 218-21. 10.1111/j.2042-3306.1999.tb05221.x.
- de Cocq P., van Weeren P.R., Back W. Effects of girth, saddle and weight on movements of the horse. Equine Vet. J. 2004;36:758–763. doi: 10.2746/0425164044848000
- de Cocq P, Prinsen H, Springer NC, van Weeren PR, Schreuder M, Muller M, van Leeuwen JL. The effect of rising and sitting trot on back movements and head-neck position of the horse. Equine Vet J. 2009 May;41(5):423-7. doi: 10.2746/042516409x371387. PMID: 19642400.
- De Cocq, P., Duncker, A. M., Clayton, H. M., Bobbert, M. F., Müller, M., & van Leeuwen, J. L. (2010). Vertical forces on the horse's back in sitting and rising trot. Journal of Biomechanics, 43(4), 627–631. https://doi.org/10.1016/j.jbiomech.2009.10.036
- Peham, Christian & Kotschwar, A.B. & Borkenhagen, B. & Kuhnke, Sandra & Molsner, J. & Baltacis, A.. (2010). A comparison of forces acting on the horse's back and the stability of the rider's seat in different positions at trot. The Veterinary Journal. 184. 56-59. 10.1016/j.tvjl.2009.04.007.
- Dyson, Sue & Ellis, Andrea & MacKechnie-Guire, Russell & Douglas, J. & Bondi, Anne & Harris, P.. (2019). The influence of rider:horse bodyweight ratio and rider-horse-saddle fit on equine gait and behaviour: A pilot study. Equine Veterinary Education. 32. 10.1111/eve.13085.
- Gunst, S., Dittmann, M. T., Arpagaus, S., Roepstorff, C., Latif, S. N., Klaassen, B., Pauli, C. A., Bauer, C. M., & Weishaupt, M. A. (2019). Influence of Functional Rider and Horse Asymmetries on Saddle Force Distribution During Stance and in Sitting Trot. Journal of equine veterinary science, 78, 20–28. https://doi.org/10.1016/j.jevs.2019.03.215
- Hampson, Alexandra & Randle, Hayley. (2015). The influence of an 8-week rider core fitness program on the equine back at sitting trot. International Journal of Performance Analysis in Sport. 15. 1145-1159. 10.1080/24748668.2015.11868858.
- Douglas, Jenni & Price, Mike & Peters, Derek. (2012). A systematic review of physiological fitness and biomechanical performance in equestrian athletes. Comparative Exercise Physiology. 8. 53-62. 10.3920/CEP12003.

THANK YOU

A big thank you to the horses, owners, riders and colleagues who allowed us to share their stories and work within this book, your contribution is greatly appreciated! Please note, in many cases we changed some details to protect the identity of horses and owners, but overall the stories are real cases.

Thank you to you, the reader for purchasing this book. We hope you now have more confidence in understanding how to best structure your training programs to help reduce the risk of injury.

To learn more about us and what we do, or to ask us a question, you can find us at:

 www.equimotion.com.au and www.eq-active.com

 info@equimotion.com.au

 @equimotionau and @eq.active

 @equimotion_au and @eq.active

INDEX

a
Acute:chronic workload (ACWR) 74-81
Aerobic fitness 16-18, 28-32, 66, 106, 110-112
Anaerobic fitness 17
Asymmetry 7, 12-13, 22-33, 45-47, 83, 99, 134, 151

b
Back health 126, 128-130
Back pain 23, 41, 140-141, 143, 146

c
Canter 111-112
Circles 114

d
Deep digital flexor tendon (DDFT) 10, 12-13, 55-56
Detraining 64-67
Dynamic mobilisation exercises (DMEs) 41, 96-98, 119-121
Dynamic stretching 41, 94-95

e
Endurance 16, 18, 28, 32-35, 151

f
Fetlock 9, 13, 55-56, 110, 117-121, 148, 151
Flexibility 16, 20, 40-41, 93-95
FITTP 26-27, 42
Functional measures 90

g
Gallop 112-113
Goldilocks principle 58-59
Gradients 105-106, 128, 137-138

h
Hip 7, 99, 105-106, 124, 130, 133
Hock 8, 13, 40, 89, 105-106
Hoof 10-14, 56, 107-108, 128
Hypermobility 20, 58

i
Interval training 32-33

j
Jumping 115-116

k
Kissing spines 130, 146

l
Lameness 10-11, 23, 46, 83-84, 145, 150
Ligaments 7, 10, 12, 29, 55-58, 123-124, 130
Load 54-56, 68-73
Long and low 36, 130

m
Mobility 16, 20, 41-42, 118-119
Motor control 16, 24
Muscles 6, 9, 20, 56, 58, 61-62, 93=94, 96, 99, 105-106, 109-110, 112, 123-127, 130-131, 133-135, 140

n
Neck health 127-130

o
Overuse injury 57-58

p
Pain 85-89
Palmar/plantar angles 11
Pelvis 7, 58, 83-84, 123, 133
Poles 42, 99-104
Posture 11, 58, 89, 119, 129-139
Power 16, 19, 36-39, 93-95, 116
Progressive overload 58-60
Proprioception 16, 21, 107
Protein 63, 128, 135

r
Rate of perceived exertion (RPE) 26, 69-71, 75, 78-80
Rest and recovery 61-63
Rider influence 148-150, 152
Rider fitness & symmetry 151-152

s
Sacroiliac joint 7, 89
Saddle fit 65, 86, 126, 128, 134-135, 140-144, 150
Skill development 16, 24, 49-52
SMART goals 43-44
Speed 128-29, 68, 109-114
Spine 7, 123-126, 128, 130-133
Straightness 16, 22, 45-48
Strength 16, 19, 36-37, 40
Stretching 40-41, 93-96
Surface 83, 107-108
Suspensory apparatus 55-56, 110
Superficial digital flexor tendon (SDFT) 55-56, 108
Symmetry 16, 22-23, 45-48, 96, 151-152

t
Thoracic sling 6, 110, 119, 130, 135-137
Topline 126, 131-139, 144
Trot 109-111

w
Walk 109, 111

www.ingramcontent.com/pod-product-compliance
Lightning Source LLC
Chambersburg PA
CBHW042024100526
44587CB00029B/4294